Twayne's Filmmakers Series

Warren French
EDITOR

Roman Polanski

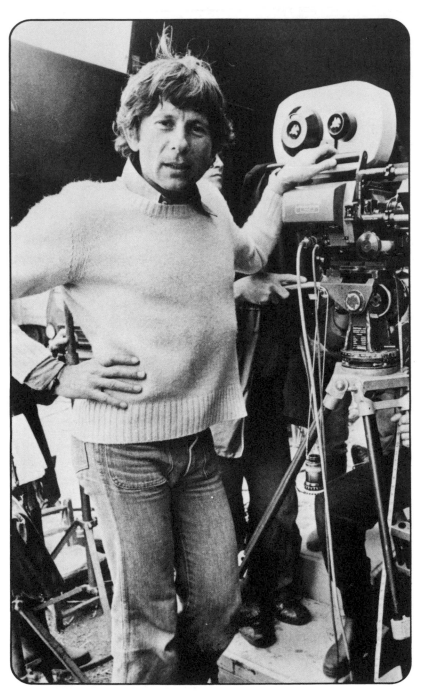

Roman Polanski on the set of Tess. *Courtesy of the* Chicago Reader.

Roman Polanski

VIRGINIA WRIGHT WEXMAN
University of Illinois, Chicago

BOSTON

Twayne Publishers

1985

Roman Polanski

is first published in 1985 by Twayne Publishers
A Division of G. K. Hall & Company
A publishing subsidiary of ITT
Copyright © 1985 by G. K. Hall & Company
All Rights Reserved

Printed on permanent/durable acid-free paper
and bound in the United States of America

First Printing, April 1985

Book Production by Marne B. Sultz

Library of Congress Cataloging in Publication Data

Wexman, Virginia Wright.
Roman Polanski.

(Twayne's filmmakers series)
Bibliography: p. 139
Filmography: p. 141
Includes index.
1. Polanski, Roman.   I. Title.   II. Series.
PN1998.A3P5849   1985   791.43'0233'0924   84-22531
ISBN 0-8057-9296-1

Contents

About the Author

VIRGINIA WRIGHT WEXMAN received her B.A., M.A., and Ph.D. from the University of Chicago, where she specialized in American literature, popular culture, and film. While in graduate school, she worked extensively in journalism and broadcasting. Since 1976 she has taught literature, media studies, and film at the University of Illinois, Chicago, where she is currently associate professor of English.

In addition to scholarly articles, Professor Wexman has written *Roman Polanski: A Guide to References and Resources* and *Robert Altman: A Guide to References and Resources*, both in collaboration with Gretchen Bisplinghoff. She is also the editor of *Cinema Journal*. Currently she is at work on a book dealing with screen acting.

Editor's Foreword

A FEW EPISODES in Roman Polanski's private life have made him so much the property of gossip sheets in this country and abroad that his achievements as a filmmaker have too often been overlooked. While *Chinatown* (1974), which Virginia Wright Wexman considers his best work to date, remains well known through repertoire revival houses and his most recent film, *Tess* (1979), has been a critical and box-office success, a number of his other films, including *Cul-de-Sac, Dance of the Vampires, Macbeth, What?* and *The Tenant,* have received at best limited distribution in the United States, so that knowledge of the development of his career has been fragmentary.

Since, whatever else one may think about Polanski's films, they provide, as this book explains, one of the most serious and disturbing cinematic records of the "cultural and aesthetic disorientation" of the post–World War II world, they occupy a unique place among not just the films, but the arts in general in our time. Thoroughly familiar with Polanski's whole body of work and the scattered international criticism of it, Professor Wexman is able to provide an analytical framework for understanding the director as a symbol for his times as well as an autonomous artist with a kind of vision that is rare in commercial cinema.

This is a particularly appropriate time for such a work, because, although Polanski is only in his early fifties, his own future and his future reputation are difficult to foresee. Professor Wexman suggests the way in which his shift from the bizarre fringes of contemporary life in his earlier films to probing the past in his film version of Thomas Hardy's novel *Tess of the D'Urbervilles* signals a new maturity. *Tess* certainly displays an ability to produce lush, epical evocations of Victorian life that are akin to the exciting work of the first important generation of Australian filmmakers; but we can only speculate whether this Victorian revaluation will flourish or fade along with other historical restorations that have become fashionable contemporary life-styles.

Time may prove this book to be the record of a stormy and uneven, but at times spectacularly brilliant, career or simply the thorough review needed at this time of the "modernist" years in Polanski's career as he enters in midlife upon another phase. In either event, it well serves the aims of this series by providing an account of the way an artist with a dark vision has brought to the screen a series of films that draw upon the often superficial traditions of popular horror films to provide a frightening record of the disastrous consequences of the modernist alienation that has pervaded Western culture during the twentieth century.

W.F.

Preface

ROMAN POLANSKI'S PERSONAL LIFE has made him so notorious that it has been difficult for commentators to see his films as anything more than expressions of his private problems and obsessions. I have focused here primarily on the films themselves, however, following the orientation of Ivan Butler's useful 1970 study *The Cinema of Roman Polanski* (New York: A. S. Barnes; London: A. Zwemmer). For readers who wish to understand more about the connections between the films and Polanski's private life, Barbara Leaming's recent biography, *Polanski: The Filmmaker as Voyeur* (New York: Simon & Schuster, 1982), provides a wealth of well-researched information that complements my own analyses of the films. Polanski's autobiography *Roman* (New York: William Morrow, 1984) provides especially useful supplementary information on his formative years.

The present study views Polanski's oeuvre in terms of its relationship to his audience. His alienating style expresses a vision of the artist and his public as adversaries bound together by mutual hostility. Though Polanski's early short film *When Angels Fall* addressed the concerns of the Polish people, his subsequent modernist-influenced works were aimed at an elite international audience of critics who were attracted by their abstractness and their cynicism. By contrast, the director's horror films, intended for a wide public, addressed formulaic conventions that are deeply rooted in specific cultural patterns. Polanski's mature works, *Macbeth*, *Chinatown*, and *Tess*, synthesize all of these influences, enriching the appeal they make to cultural mythologies by alluding to cultures of the past as well as the present. Because of their historical context, these later films involve their audiences more deeply than the earlier ones could ever do, for they assault long-standing attitudes toward particular social practices involving issues of class, race, and gender relations. Polanski's exploration of the cultural mechanisms through which such prejudices are deployed has recently led him to adopt a more sympathetic stance toward the audience he once baited. Thus, in *Tess*, the desires of spectator and filmmaker harmonize in a new way.

The book begins with a chapter considering the broad aesthetic and political significance of Polanski's early years in Poland. He was active in the avant-garde theater as well as in student film groups. The personal hardships he suffered as a Polish Jew in World War II show up in a cynicism about political and religious issues and in a complex sympathy toward social outsiders. Polanski has tried to escape his cultural roots by embracing an internationally comprehensible cinematic style, but at a deep level his Polish heritage has decisively shaped his attitude toward his art.

The second chapter examines the influence of two important modernist movements, absurdism and surrealism, on Polanski's shorts and on such full-length features as *Knife in the Water, Cul-de-Sac*, and *What?* These stylized and abstract films are the director's most personal statements, made under conditions of relative freedom. They develop themes of power, victimization, and sexuality that Polanski would elaborate more fully in later works.

Polanski's horror films, *Repulsion, Rosemary's Baby, The Tenant*, and the lighthearted *Dance of the Vampires*, grow out of commercial and popular traditions of cinema. Unlike the modernist films, these often focus on specific, realistic environments and explore the inner workings of the protagonists' psychologies. Though sensational, they nevertheless engage serious aesthetic, social, and psychological dilemmas, not the least of which is the question of why we enjoy watching such films in the first place. Chapter 3 treats these four films together as Polanski's survey of the kinds of power and pleasure there are to be derived from the horror formula.

Chapter 4 is on *Macbeth*. While clearly a subject that fits what by now can be recognized as Polanski's major themes, it stands apart from the horror films as such. The psychological terror so familiar a part of other Polanski films is here related to what Jan Kott calls the "nightmare of history." In this work for the first time Polanski considers issues of social change and stability.

Such historical considerations and the experience of working with popular genres served Polanski well in the making of *Chinatown*, the subject of chapter 5. Though it was produced in an atmosphere of controversy and chaos, most critics, including myself, see it as Polanski's richest film. *Chinatown* involves the audience in the psychology of its hero by playing on the expectations intrinsic to the hard-boiled detective formula. At the same time, it relates the generic experience to more universalized mythic patterns and ultimately to the "myth" of historical progress.

Finally, the sixth chapter, on *Tess*, examines how the director adapts Hardy's tragic novel to present a more optimistic vision of the possibilities of sexual fulfillment than he has ever done before. This new treatment of sexuality is accompanied by a more accepting attitude toward his audience. The film's nostalgic and harmonious ambience recalls a time before modernism had alienated human beings from their surroundings and from each other.

Because Polanski's relationship with his audience has been complex, and because it has played such a major role in the development of his art, I have not treated his oeuvre as the expression of an idiosyncratic sensibility that transcends the conditions under which he has worked. Though he has a strong personal vision that he imposes on all his films, this vision has been modified and deepened by the exigencies of filmmaking itself. The economic realities of the film industry, which have forced him to appeal to a large public, have had a beneficial effect on his art. They have encouraged him to lay aside eccentric personal preoccupations and to communicate fantasies that have a cultural as well as personal significance. Collaboration has had a similar effect, forcing the director to synthesize the contributions of different talents. Ironically, the director's most cherished projects, made under conditions of the greatest freedom, are often his worst. The romantic image of the artist as a free spirit whose eccentricities should be indulged does not hold true for Polanski. The course of his career argues that the creative compromises required by collaboration and by popular taste may actually contribute to artistic development.

For the successful completion of this study, I am indebted to many sources. John Cawelti supervised my dissertation on hard-boiled detective films, which included a chapter on *Chinatown* in which I first began to formulate my ideas on Polanski. Ron Gottesmann offered me an opportunity to publish my research on the director as part of the G. K. Hall Reference Guide series, a volume I coauthored with Gretchen Bisplinghoff. Other friends and colleagues have generously read and criticized various parts of the present manuscript: Marvin Mirsky, Jerry Carlson, Gerald Mast, Linda Williams, Judy Gardiner, and Robert Carringer, among others. More general discussions with members of my department, especially Jonathan Arac, Clark Hulse, Sandra Lieb, Sheldon Liebman, Ned Lukacher, Leah Marcus, Ann Matsuhashi, Christian Messenger, and David Spurr, have been invaluable in shaping the theoretical underpinnings of my analyses. A travel grant and a summer research fellowship from the University of Illinois at Chicago provided me with much-needed financial support. Richard Pettingill at the University of Chicago Film Study Center and Emily Sieger at the Library of Congress were extremely helpful in arranging for me to re-view many of Polanski's films, and Elizabeth Davidson-Ludicky provided invaluable assistance in obtaining permissions and frame enlargements.

For my husband, John Huntington, who has made extraordinary contributions both to my work and to my life, my feelings go far deeper than gratitude. This book is dedicated to him.

VIRGINIA WRIGHT WEXMAN

University of Illinois, Chicago

Chronology

1933	Roman Polanski born of Polish-Jewish parents in the Bastille section of Paris on August 18.
1936	The Polanskis return to Poland, homeland of the director's father.
1940	Escapes to the countryside; his parents are taken to concentration camps.
1949	His father returns to Cracow and enrolls the boy in a technical school.
1949–1953	Begins to act in radio plays, then in the theater.
1950	Transfers to art school.
1954	Rejected at the State Acting School and the Comedians' School; then accepted at the State Film School on the recommendation of Antoni Bohdziewicz, a faculty member who had worked with Polanski in the theater. Acts in *A Generation*, directed by Andrzej Wajda.
1956	Poznan uprising. Wladyslaw Gomulka named First Secretary of the Polish Communist party. Liberalization of Polish censorship.
1958	Directs *Two Men and a Wardrobe* (short film).
1959	Marries Barbara Kwiatkowska (stage name: Barbara Lass) and directs her in short, *When Angels Fall*, made for his diploma at Lodz. French director Jean Drot visits Poland and introduces Polanski to Gerard Brach, his future scriptwriting collaborator.
1961	Travels to Paris and makes shorts *The Fat and the Lean* and *Mammals*, the latter of which was later completed in Poland. Divorces Barbara Kwiatkowska.

1962   Directs first feature, *Knife in the Water.*

1963–   Writes script for *Cul-de-Sac* with Gerard Brach.
1964

1965   Makes *Repulsion* in England.

1966   Films *Cul-de-Sac* in England.

1967   Directs *Dance of the Vampires (The Fearless Vampire Killers)* in England. Sharon Tate stars.

1968   Marries Sharon Tate. Comes to the United States to direct *Rosemary's Baby.* Resigns from the jury at the Cannes Film Festival out of sympathy with the French student uprisings.

1969   Prepares script for *Day of the Dolphin,* which he is scheduled to direct. August 9, receives call in London informing him that his wife (then eight-and-one-half-months pregnant) and three friends have been murdered at his home in Los Angeles. Later it is discovered that members of the Charles Manson cult performed the killings.

1971   Directs *Macbeth* in England.

1973   Directs *What?* in Italy.

1974   Directs *Chinatown* in the United States and Berg's opera *Lulu* in Spoleto, Italy.

1976   Directs and stars in *The Tenant* in Paris.

1979   Arrested in Los Angeles on charges of unlawful sexual intercourse with a thirteen-year-old girl; sentenced to ninety days in prison for observation. Flees the country in order to avoid further criminal proceedings. Directs *Tess* in France.

1981   Directs stage production of Peter Shaffer's *Amadeus* in Warsaw, and plays the role of Mozart.

1984   Publishes autobiography. Begins work on *Pirates* in Tunesia.

1

The Polish Experience

Backgrounds

Interviewer: As a Polish director who has made perhaps a half-dozen feature films, each made farther and farther west of Poland, may I ask what has brought you this far from home?

Polanski: Well, I don't know. I do things which I like. If suddenly you say there is something interesting to do in Alaska I would go and do it. I'm going further and further from Poland. As you know, the earth is round—so who knows, maybe I'll come back from the other side.[1]

MORSE PECKHAM WRITES: "Art is the re-inforcement of the capacity to endure disorientation so that real and significant problems may emerge."[2] Of all major directors, probably none has produced a body of work so truly cosmopolitan as Roman Polanski. Fluent in five languages, he has made films in Poland, Italy, England, France, and the United States; and he has lived for extended periods of time in the latter three countries. He was born in France in 1933, but he returned with his parents to their native Poland three years later, and he lived there to the age of twenty-one. Though it is easy for critics on this side of the Atlantic to overlook the crucial role Polanski's early years in Poland played in shaping his art, during that time, the future director absorbed many of the cultural and aesthetic influences current in postwar Poland. It is this basic experience that forms the core out of which all of his work has grown. Though Polanski may have become a cultural cosmopolitan, he is first of all a Pole.

In an article on the Polish cinema, Gene Moskowitz records the comment of one of Polanski's countrymen to the effect that Poland is "a fine nation but badly located."[3] Given their historical affinity with the West, Poles felt trapped and betrayed when, after the debacle of Nazism, the western allies decided to barter Poland off to its traditional enemy Russia. Historically, Poland has been overrun by almost every country in Europe; and during World War I, Poles were drafted into the Austrian, German, and Russian armies.

Poland *by Jacek Malchiewski (1914).*

1

Poles feel displaced not only geographically but also chronologically. Film historians Mira and Antonin Liehm have referred to "the dream of a great Poland that keeps reappearing in Polish history, only to end in repeated tragedy."[4] Polanski's Polish background has conditioned him to see the past as an endlessly repeated series of catastrophes. His view of history is rooted in the repeated frustrations suffered by his homeland in its attempt to achieve its dream of greatness.

The Polish dream became a nightmare during World War II when millions of Poles were killed. The degree to which Polanski himself was scarred by this experience would be hard to overestimate. At eight, the future director watched the walling off of the Cracow ghetto. Escaping alone to the country, he was later shot at by Nazi troopers for target practice. As a Jew in a Catholic culture, he was aware not only of the oppression of his people fostered by the prevailing religious beliefs in Poland, but also of the more virulent anti-Semitism, which led to his mother's death at Auschwitz. Later, under communism, instances of racial bigotry continued: two of his former Jewish teachers at Lodz lost their positions in 1968, reportedly as the result of anti-Semitic sentiment.[5] Such early experiences explain, at least in part, the bitter satires of religion in most of Polanski's films. By age fourteen, he claims he was an atheist, and his work is invariably critical of Christianity—particularly Catholicism. At the same time, however, his films reveal a fascination with the pagan superstitions that existed alongside orthodox Roman Catholicism among the rural peasants with whom he lived. The vampire folklore that is affectionately mocked in the 1967 *Dance of the Vampires* has its roots in this region.[6]

After the war, Poles confronted another threat to their culture in the form of Communist repression. The specter of regimentation and censorship posed by a nationalized film industry undoubtedly contributed to the aggressive, rebellious tone of much of Polanski's work. His first completed short, *Two Men and a Wardrobe* (1958), pits its two protagonists against a conformist culture in which even the junkyard is composed of rows of identical old barrels. Polanski came of age at a moment in Polish history just after the successful Poznan uprising of October 1956, when the burden of conformism to state-defined values was growing lighter. The relative freedom he briefly enjoyed, however, ended abruptly in 1963 when the First Secretary of the Polish Communist party, Wladyslaw Gomulka himself, denounced Polanski's first feature, *Knife in the Water* (1961), as inconsistent with the values of the socialist state.

Considering the psychic burden Polanski's past has placed on him, his overt rejection of political, religious, and nationalistic commitment is understandable. "I guess I'm an anarchist," he once told an interviewer.[7] And his films communicate a deep despair about the potential of any political, moral, or emotional commitment to make a difference to people's lives. Instead, he gave his allegiance to art, which reminded him of happier aspects of his childhood. As a virtual orphan during World War II, he developed a voracious appetite for movies and plays to escape an intolerable existence.[8] Through fantasy, he was able to forget, if only temporarily and partially, the atrocities surrounding him. "If there is any Gothic tendency in my cinema," he has said, "it is rather nostalgia for things that gave me so much pleasure as a child, such as *Snow White and the Seven Dwarfs* or *Robinhood.*"[9]

Early in his life, Polanski came to value filmmaking itself above anything else. "I always wanted to make films," he has recalled, "as far back as I can remember."[10] As a young adolescent, he began to act, first on radio, then in the theater, and finally in films. After studying painting and sculpture, he enrolled in the renowned Polish film school at Lodz. A rigorous five-year program followed, beginning with a year of still photography and ending with the direction of a 16mm short film that made use of sophisticated techniques of cinematography and editing. During these years, the aspiring director developed a command of the craft of filmmaking that has invariably impressed his colleagues wherever he has worked. He remembers interminable student debates at Lodz over the merits of different directors and styles. "An important part of our education was a baroque wooden stairway where we would sit for hours arguing about films, which sometimes we were screening all day and all night," the director has recalled. "Occasionally, the discussions became rather heated. In fact, I have a scar over my eye from one of them."[11]

If social and political traditions have provided the substance of Polanski's fantasies, the aesthetic traditions that this education was built on have dictated their form. He grew up in Cracow, the most historic and beautiful city in Poland. As an art student, he could hardly have avoided the influence of the powerful romantic and surrealist strains that have marked the development of Polish painting over the past two centuries. Besides sharpening his visual sensitivity, his years in art school also provided him with a background in art history, which he often draws upon to expand the scope of meaning in his filmic texts.

As a child actor, Polanski must have absorbed the impact of new movements in the Polish theater, where he spent many hours in the balcony as well as on the stage. Though the tradition of the Polish avant-garde theater, as described by the critic Daniel Gerould, was "a lonely, private, prophetic one,"[12] nonetheless, it never abrogated its connections to the culture that had nurtured it. "Centered on the exceptional individual— intellectual or artist—and his relation to the masses, the Polish Avant-Garde is preeminently a theater of revolution, social upheaval, and historical crisis, conceived in metaphoric terms."[13]

This tradition has deep roots in the romantic drama of the nineteenth century. Writers like Adam Mickiewicz, Juliusz Slowacki, and Stanislaw Wyspianski created mystical, dreamlike works that have been seen as

forerunners to the surrealist art of the twentieth century.[14] In more recent
times this tradition has merged with that of absurdism, most importantly
in the work of Stanislaw Ignacy Witkiewicz (known as Witacy), and Witold
Gombrowicz.[15] Currently the most prominent playwright working in the
Polish avant-garde theater is Slowomir Mrozek, the author of *Tango*
(1965), whom Polanski knew during his artistic apprenticeship. Because of
their abstractness, absurdist plays that denied meaning and value were
well formulated to express the mood of postwar Poland.[16] Without referring directly to the political realities that had occasioned them, such plays
expressed allegorically the humiliation and trauma the Poles had suffered.
Absurdism thus could speak to the Polish experience in an acceptably
apolitical manner while at the same time appealing to an international
audience.

The most powerful force in the Polish contemporary theater is the director Jerzy Grotowski, whose groundbreaking production of Ionesco's
The Chairs was staged at the Stary Theater in Cracow in 1957. Shortly
thereafter, Grotowski revived the early Polish works of Mickiewicz, Slowacki, and Wispianski.

Grotowski's minimalist or "poor" theater (as he calls it) draws on theories of myth and the unconscious, which were first sketched out by Wit-
kacy but bear a close affinity with ideas espoused by the French surrealist
Antonin Artaud.[17] Like Artaud, Grotowski's aim is to go beyond ordinary
civilized activity, or what he calls the "life mask," to what he considers the
primitive and irrational principles behind human behavior. These, he assumes, have been repressed. Because he is interested in myth and the
unconscious rather than "ordinary" rational behavior, Grotowski, along
with Artaud, has emphasized non-naturalistic acting styles geared toward
"eliminating those elements of 'natural' behavior which obscure pure impulse."[18] We shall see a similar commitment to "pure impulse" in Polanski
as he explores the mechanics of the unconscious in his interiorized studies
of madness. He also relies heavily on cultural myths in such films as *Dance
of the Vampires* and *Chinatown* (1974). And the mannered acting in most
of his films, from *Cul-de-Sac* (1966) to *Chinatown*, reveals Polanski's Gro-
towski-like desire to probe beneath naturalistic surfaces.

But most important to an understanding of the meaning of Polanski's
Polish experience is Grotowski's emphasis on active involvement between
actors and audiences as a means of breaking through the "life mask." "The
essential concern is finding the proper spectator-actor relationship for
each type of performance and embodying the decision in physical arrange-
ments."[19] Polanski's films enact such relationships directly and aggressively. The spectator's position as a voyeur is often alluded to by shots framed
by keyholes or other apertures. Moreover, outbreaks of violence are often
aimed directly at the audience. Early in *Knife in the Water* a journalist
lashes out at his wife while directly facing the spectator—in close-up; in

Chinatown, a corrupt law-enforcement official has his skull smashed against the camera, and in *Repulsion* (1965), a murderess wields her weapon, a candlestick, directly in front of the lens. Such moments are the cinematic equivalent of Grotowski's stage devices, which insist that the audience participate in the performance.

While absorbing this aesthetic of the Polish avant-garde, Polanski was also influenced by a more "grass roots" theatrical tradition that had grown among the young people of Poland. During the mid-1950s students began forming amateur theatrical troupes to perform skits that relied on mime, parody, fantasy, and many techniques borrowed from film. The most renowned was the Bim Bom troupe. Touring abroad to international acclaim, the group also played engagements around Poland to large, diverse audiences. Several of its members who were personal friends of Polanski's during this time, including Zbigniew Cybuluski, were later to achieve fame in the legitimate Polish theater and in films. Openly critical of the prevailing Communist regime, all of the skits performed by the Bim Bom troupe had a common theme. They centered on the conflict between characters called *roosters*, modeled after state functionaries, and *organ grinders*, designed to represent the artist as an everyman figure. The artist-hero was invariably "the Chaplinesque little man, the powerless nobody in an alien world, as much at sea in the modern world as the nearly extinct great individualist, but more humble, guiltless, and guileless. He is simply a lost cog in the machine. In the new mass society, the anonymous, faceless hero is the victim of the state that crushes him while claiming to serve him."[20] Polanski's shorts, and in particular *The Fat and the Lean* (1960), with its Chaplinesque servant crushed by his "protector," owe much to this model.

Like most other Polish filmmakers, Polanski experienced the presence of the official doctrine of Soviet socialist realism, whose principles had been set out at the Pan-Soviet literary congress of 1934. In this tradition "introspection and interest in imaginative stylistic devices is condemned, while the portrayal of man in his everyday life and of the virtues of socialism is encouraged." After the war, the Polish film industry was nationalized, and in 1948 the National Film Academy was established at Lodz. In 1949, Polish filmmakers were explicitly instructed to further the goals of the Communist state by portraying "the positive hero of the new Poland."[21] This "realism" served the interests of the state by offering a progressive view of history, idealized proletarian heroes, and the values of optimism, cooperation, and antimaterialism. Obviously, in the context of a nationalized film industry such as that of Poland, such principles operated as powerful forces.

Nonetheless, the standards were challenged. With their romantic attachment to the past, Poles had always encouraged historical films. Polanski thus comes quite naturally by his recent tendency to dwell on the past (in *Macbeth* (1971), *Chinatown*, and *Tess* (1979)). Moreover, a long and honorable tradition of documentary filmmaking developed. The 1920s saw the formation of the Society of Devotees of the Artistic Film (START), which had much in common with the Italian neorealist movement.[22] In addition, the avant-garde theatrical style became an increasingly powerful influence on Polish filmmakers, an influence incompatible with socialist realism. Out of this style came introspective, expressionistic works, the best known of which include Jerzy Kawalerowicz's *Mother Joan of the Angels* (1961); Walerian Borowszyk's *Story of Sin* (1974); Wojcieck Has's *Saragossa Manuscript* (1965); and Jerzy Skolomowski's trilogy *Identification Marks: None* (1964), *Walkover* (1965), and *Barrier* (1966).

As a result of the Poznan uprising of 1956, Polish moviemakers felt freer to express these predilections, although by so doing they largely cut themselves off from their colleagues in the East European bloc. In 1957, at a conference of Eastern European filmmakers held at Prague, the main spokesman condemned the new Polish films as "hostile to the socialist system."[23] Thereafter, the films of the Polish school were rarely shown in other Communist countries. This adversarial situation was a major stimulant to the group at Lodz. In September 1954, Jerzy Toeplitz, director of the Film Academy in which the young Polanski was then a student, publicly condemned the simplistic approach of socialist realism. Together with Jerzy Bossak, head of the documentary production unit at Lodz, as well as others, Toeplitz produced films that dealt with social and political problems in sober, naturalistic terms. From 1954 to 1956, Bossak originated a "black series" of documentaries, presenting harsh political and social realities that undermined the sanguine optimism of socialist realism. That Polanski inherited the recalcitrance of his teachers and colleagues toward the values of socialist realism is clear in his first feature, *Knife in the Water* (1962), which subtly undermines the official filmmaking aesthetics under which he was working.

At the same time that Polanski adopted the rebellious spirit of these teachers, however, he differed from them in his emphasis on isolated individuals rather than large social panoramas. This approach followed that of Andrzej Wajda, who was engaged during the late 1950s in making psychological, symbolic films that exposed unattractive aspects of the Polish resistance during World War II. One of these, *A Generation* (1955), features a performance by Polanski in the role of a young member of a Communist resistance group. Wajda's decision to focus on disaffected young people in this film was typical of the concerns of many Polish filmmakers of the period, who were preoccupied with the devastating effects of the war and postwar environments on Polish youth. The plight of alienated and troubled young people has continued to play an important role in the films of Polanski himself. For one of his earliest unfinished efforts, *Break Up the Dance* (1957), the student director enlisted a group of thugs to stage a disruption of a school party, as a result of which he was himself almost expelled for delinquent behavior.

Probably an even stronger influence was Andrzej Munk, another of Polanski's teachers at Lodz, who acted as something of a mentor to the aspiring young director. Munk's documentarylike methods were played against an inclination toward black humor and grotesquery in films like *Eroica* (1957) and *The Passenger* (1961, unfinished) as well as *Bad Luck* (1959), for which Polanski served as assistant director. Both *The Passenger* and the second episode of *Eroica* are set in prisoner-of-war camps, where the complex power relationships among the prisoners and their captors are explored with considerable irony.

Polanski's cinema often documents similar themes of dominance and oppression in less politicized settings. Though his own wartime experiences could have provided ample material for grotesque portrayals of war of the sort produced by Munk, he has never shown any interest in exploiting his life cinematically in this literally autobiographical way. Instead, his most personal films are more likely to be directly inspired by artistic models than by human experience. Polanski's films are fantasies; but they are also about fantasies. In his best work, it is through fantasy that he achieves the distance necessary to reimagine the cultural and psychological traumas of his youth. In this sense, all his films are Polish. Though he has overtly rejected the influence of his cultural roots, at a deeper level his past remains a powerful force in his art.

The Dilemma of Polish Culture: *When Angels Fall*

Polanski completed only one film in which the cultural and aesthetic influences of his Polish education were explicitly expressed, *When Angels Fall* (1959). In this twenty-two-minute film, an old woman who serves as an attendant in a public washroom remembers her past life as a peasant in the Polish countryside. After having been seduced by a soldier from a passing regiment, she bore a son, who developed a malicious temperament and was himself eventually pressed into the army. While fighting in the war, the young man was killed by gunfire; but his mother imagines that he will return to her as an angel to take her with him to heaven.

The film alternates black-and-white sequences depicting the present with color scenes set in the past, stylistically underscoring what the story itself makes plain: the woman's memories are more exciting and attractive than her present existence. And, as the film progresses, the color gradually fades, even from her memories, which appear more and more in the form of garish blotches of red against stark, drab backgrounds. Such a development suggests a view of life as a process of decay rather than development, a view corroborated by the increasingly melancholy music supplied by Krzysztof Komeda (who, until his death in 1969, contributed scores for most of Polanski's subsequent films).

In *When Angels Fall*, the young girl (played by Polanski's first wife, Barbara Kwiatkowska) is seduced only to be abandoned; subsequently we witness violent images of the war, during which the death spasms of a soldier whose legs have just been blown away are depicted with graphic specificity; and we see the death of another soldier before the old woman's son himself dies. Such a pattern of escalating violence and physical mutilation envisions human existence as a process of regression rather than maturation.

To reinforce this theme, Polanski includes rhyming shots of the peasant girl looking out her window. At first, gazing at the passing regiment, she is flanked by a sunflower blooming outside. Later, though, as she looks out on her young son, who is beating a frog with a stick, her troubled expression is complemented by the same sunflower, now dried and withered. This image of a window entrapping characters and providing a frame that limits and defines their vision reappears in Polanski's later films, most conspicuously in *The Tenant* (1976) and in the shot of the young heroine peering longingly in through a window that was used to publicize the 1979 *Tess*.

In *When Angels Fall* this portrayal of regression and entrapment applies not only to the old woman herself but also to her culture. What makes *When Angels Fall* different from the films that immediately follow it is Polanski's willingness to express the social as well as personal implications of this vision. The old woman's memories are presented as being, in part, the memories of Poland. The public men's washroom in which she works is elaborately and inappropriately festooned with an eclectic pastiche of ornamentation that recalls the past glories of Polish art. And Polanski himself has verified that many of the old woman's memories are shaped by the traditions of nineteenth-century Polish genre painting, in which military, religious, and patriotic themes were all glorified.[24] To contrast with the fullness and splendor of the Polish past, Polanski includes a coldly officious Polish bureaucrat, who inspects the washroom and treats the old woman as another meter to be read.

Though the drabness and indignities of the present are incontrovertible, the splendors of the past are, in some sense, illusory. Polanski makes it plain that the woman has embellished her memories by distorting ugly reality to conform to the sentimentalized views of Polish history familiar to her through popular art. Certain images animate the old woman's memories because they call up her sentimentalized notions of romance and heroism, and the memories themselves take the form of miniature artistic constructs, which are based as much on popular convention as on historical fact. Thus the girl's seducer appears to her as a dashing young cavalryman out of a storybook. And her son's venal nature (revealed by many of

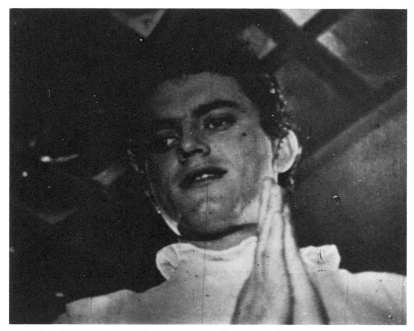

When Angels Fall *alludes to the iconography of popular Polish romantic painting in its portrayal of angels returning to earth. Frame enlargement.*

the film's details) is redeemed by his "heroic" martyrdom, which she pictures in highly stylized terms, as well as by his return to earth as an angel, another image popularized in Polish romantic painting.

One well-known Polish painting that probably served as a specific model for the image of the young girl's seduction is Jacek Malchiewski's *Poland*. In it a young man embraces the legs of a woman in much the same way as the soldier embraces those of his peasant mistress in Polanski's film. If the old woman is thereby pictured as an emblem of her country, the behavior of her son—ungrateful, petty, and self-destructive—suggests that the sons of Poland have brought about their own downfall through ignoble and ill-advised actions in the face of adversity. In one wartime episode, the son stupidly shoots a German soldier who wishes to befriend him when they are trapped freezing together during a battle, thereby offering a chilling condemnation of Polish inability to seize opportunities to make helpful alliances when these are offered them. Given Polanski's early experiences as well as the course of modern history, it is not surprising that he should harbor such an aggressive and self-punitive nihilism. What makes *When Angels Fall* so unusual in relation to his other early projects,

The pose of the soldier grasping the legs of a young peasant girl in When Angels Fall *is strikingly similar to the pose of the two figures in Malchiewski's* Poland. *Frame enlargement.*

however, is his willingness in it to see his despair within the context of the history of a particular culture, in this case his own.

When Angels Fall was Polanski's diploma film at Lodz. After having already received considerable international recognition for *Two Men and a Wardrobe* in 1956, however, he found that *When Angels Fall* was almost totally ignored. Thereafter, he returned to the abstract, "international" style that appealed to the influential coterie of critics in the West. In an interview with Wajda in 1969, he confirmed his commitment to internationalism. "What Poland has given me is inestimable," he said. "But my trips to other countries and the discoveries of their literatures have also been invaluable. If I had no understanding of what went on outside of Poland, I could never have continued to make films because the ones I made wouldn't have been good enough."[25]

Polanski's later development has shown, however, that he did not give up the portrayal of cultural processes. Eventually he brought the examination of society and history that characterized *When Angels Fall* to films that depicted other cultures, thus providing his later work with a perspective that is rich and sophisticated, yet distanced and oblique. *When Angels*

Fall can be thought of, in fact, as the Polish version of *Chinatown*, though the latter film deals with a culture whose traditions are better understood internationally than are Poland's and more central to the recent development of Western culture in general. By the time Polanski made *Chinatown*, he was ready for this challenge. His experiences blending avant-garde and commercial filmmaking styles in various countries had further sharpened his skills as a director even as they had given him a deeper perspective on the relationship between culture and art. With *Chinatown* Polanski has, in a sense, come back to his homeland "from the other side"—from the side, that is, of the deep and genuine encounter with culture that would probably have been denied him if he had remained in his homeland. It was first necessary, however, for him to escape both the subject matter and style of Polish art, to be "disoriented," in order for his work to transform his early fantasies into a precise yet universal vision.

2
The Escape into Style: Modernism

Absurdism and Surrealism: Polanski's Modernist Aesthetic

TO SPEAK OF POLANSKI is to speak of modernism. It is also to speak of the limits of modernism, for having fully embraced modernist principles, he has drawn back from them in his more recent films. The process by which this development has occurred tells us not only about the director himself but also about the future directions that could be taken by the modernist movement as a whole.[1]

As Georg Lukács and others have argued, the possibility of any meaningful, developing relationship between human beings and the societal and natural environments that nurture them is often denied by the modernist aesthetic. "This negation of history takes two different forms in modernist literature," Lukács has written. "First, the hero is strictly confined within the limits of his own experience. There is not for him—and apparently not for his creator—any pre-existent reality beyond his own self, acting upon him or being acted upon by him. Secondly, the hero himself is without personal history. He is 'thrown-into-the-world': meaninglessly, unfathomably. He does not develop through contact with the world; he neither forms nor is formed by it. The only 'development' in this literature is the gradual revelation of the human condition."[2] Given the international character of twentieth-century culture as well as its sense of temporal discontinuity, such a longing to escape from tradition is not surprising. The sense of discontinuity is expressed not only by the subject matter of twentieth-century art but also by its form. In modernist art, cogent story lines disintegrate into ambiguous open-endedness, coherent characterizations give way to opacity and capriciousness, "meaningful" themes are denied by insouciant satire and parody, and verisimilitude is qualified by fantasy. The impression of fragmentation and paradox engendered by such techniques has been identified by Susan Sontag with a mode that emphasizes stylization over style: "Stylization in a work of art, as distinct from style, reflects ambivalence (affection contradicted by contempt, admiration contradicted by irony) toward the subject matter. This

lanski, in the role of a young thug, prepares to strike the *mera in* Two Men and a Wardrobe. *Frame enlargement.*

ambivalence is handled by maintaining, through the rhetorical overlay that is stylization, a special distance from the subject."[3]

If such an approach characterizes modernism in general, it also describes a particular orientation to cinema that is recognizably Polanskian. His early work, including the shorts *Knife in the Water*, *Cul-de-Sac*, and *What?* (1973), present extreme horrors of contemporary life abstracted from the specific environmental stresses that give rise to them. His most personal work attempts to rise above national and sociological considerations. The horrors he depicts are designed as metaphysical challenges to the resiliency of the human sensibility. In a sense, his is the art of a survivor.

According to Polanski himself, the two modernist movements that have most influenced him are those of the theater of the absurd and surrealism. Both movements played an important role in the Polish avant-garde environment in which his art was formed.[4] Initially the theater of the absurd dominates his work, most obviously in his early short films. Gradually, however, surrealist elements become more prevalent, especially in the later horror films. Yet principles of both schools provide him with important generating ideas centered on issues of power and sexuality, issues that have animated his work from the beginning. At first such ideas dictate the shape of entire films. In his maturity, however, his modernist perspective creates a subtext that subtly modifies and comments on more traditional forms.

In the theater of the absurd, the nihilistic abstractions associated with modernist art take an extreme form. Absurdist drama typically features buffoonish characters carrying on laconic, nonsensical conversations amid eccentrically spare and decrepit settings. The presumption of narrative development is undercut at every turn by repetitive, entropic lines of action. Such devices grow out of a cynical, pessimistic view of a slowly dying world in which nothing can be trusted. In such a world, life must be meaningless—as must art, a corollary communicated through the extensive use of self-deprecatory burlesque and parody.

Polanski, who had been overwhelmed on seeing Samuel Beckett's *Waiting for Godot* in 1956, embraced this aesthetic wholeheartedly in his early work. In the dried-up, weed-infested garden that serves as a setting for *The Fat and the Lean*, a grossly unkempt master and his waifish servant enact a variation of the Pozzo-Lucky relationship in *Waiting for Godot*. *Knife in the Water* is a Pinteresque examination of hostilities among three people isolated on a boat in the lonely lake region of Poland. *Cul-de-Sac* features two down-at-the-heel gangsters hiding out in a castle on the sea to wait for a Godot-like figure called Katelbach, who never appears. And *What?* parodies *Alice in Wonderland*, an important precursor of the absurdist tradition.

Such references to particular absurdist models are presented in the context of visual and narrative structures built on principles of entropy rather than progression. Typically Polanski composes his frames sparsely and paces his editing slowly, thereby emptying his images and stories of content. In such an environment, characters tend to lose ground rather than gain it, often regressing to positions of total inertia at the story's conclusion. With the exception of *When Angels Fall*, all the shorts feature episodic plots built on endless variations of the same absurd situation in which things grow progressively worse with each variation. The full-length features depict more complex interactions based on the same principle. Such static repetitiveness is parodied in *Cul-de-Sac* by irritatingly monotonous music, which is, at one point, even played on a broken record. There is so little to look for and so little to wait for in Polanski's modernist films that the anomie expressed by the actions of most of the major characters seems both inescapable and interminable.

This perception of an ultimate nothingness is often symbolized in these films by the image of water, which, by its amorphous featurelessness, suggests a primal void at the center of things, a void from which human beings can only obtain a temporary and illusory escape. *Cul-de-Sac* ends with an image of the sea; *Two Men and a Wardrobe* both ends and begins with one. In *Knife in the Water*, the characters have been cast adrift on a boat. To be thus cast adrift is to recognize the fundamental ontological insecurity that prevails in a universe where nothing has solidity or value. As one of the characters in *Knife in the Water* observes, "Floating on water is nothing; it's nothing."

As the borders of this void, beaches also play an important role in many of Polanski's films, from his first short, *Two Men and a Wardrobe*, which begins and ends on a beach, to *Tess*, which departs from Thomas Hardy's original novel to include a shot of the beach at Sandbourne. If beaches symbolize the metaphysical borderland on which the action of the narrative sometimes occurs, other scenes set on land offer little respite from their barrenness. Snow-covered fields, scruffy meadows, and rocky islands are the typical settings for the modernist films, defining a world where growth and fecundity are largely absent.

In this bleak world, the transcendent aspirations of the human spirit count for little. "I don't believe man has free will," Polanski has stated. "Man's choice is always the result of his life experience."[5] His compositions reflect this negation of free will, for they tend either to be closed and constricting, communicating entrapment, like the boat's cabin in *Knife in the Water* or open and featureless, offering no guidelines or direction to their human inhabitants, like the snow-covered meadows in *Mammals* (1961). And often there are apertures such as windows and archways, teasing the characters who look through them with the possibilities of openness, while the audience, looking in through the frame, sees that their vision is, in fact, defined and restricted. In *The Fat and the Lean* the young servant gazes wistfully out the kitchen window at the seductive outlines of the distant city. And the frustrated husband in the opening scene of *Knife in the Water* looks anxiously through the windshield of his car for a means of breaking through his wife's reserve as she drives through the Polish countryside. Images like these deny the characters the freedom to discover authentic alternatives to the restricted patterns of their lives.

Despairing of human freedom, Polanski makes what Leo Braudy has called closed films, in which "everything is totally sufficient, everything fits in."[6] In such films, narrative and visual structures define and determine the characters' actions. In Polanski's work, plots typically begin and end with neatly rhyming episodes: in *Two Men and a Wardrobe* two men emerge from the sea, then return to it; at the end of *What?*, Nancy leaves the villa by means of the same elevator she uses to enter it at the outset. Such narrative framing devices make the protagonists' attempts at purposeful action appear as the expression of naive misunderstandings about the underlying absurdity of the universe in which they are caught, a universe in which all choices produce the same result. As Ivan Butler puts it, "the shape of the film itself reflects its own circular, enclosed world."[7] For similar reasons, Polanski favors framing techniques that lock his characters into tightly controlled formal patterns. In *Cul-de-Sac*, Albert watches Richard through the angular opening between the automobile windshield and the door frame. As the old woman of *When Angels Fall* descends into the public washroom where she works, she is viewed from a low angle that contrasts her frail figure with the heavy, coalescing lines of the ceiling and stairway.

The impotence of Polanski's protagonists is also expressed in the unresolved endings of his films. At the conclusion of *Knife in the Water*, the main character, stopped at a fork in the road, remains immobile behind the wheel of his car, unable to choose between the two alternatives; and at the end of *Cul-de-Sac*, the central character is stranded on a rock in the middle of a flooded causeway, similarly incapable of deciding on any future course of action. Polanski's refusal to satisfy his audience's desire for closure is related to his conviction that there are no clear solutions to the enigmas of existence. "To satisfy is an unpleasant way for me," he has said. "Satisfaction is a most unpleasant feeling."[8]

The psychological underpinnings of the absurdist sensibility have been well analyzed by two psychiatrists, Norman S. Litowitz and Kenneth M. Newman, who relate the sensationalism, fragmentation, and despair of the absurdist weltanschauung to the minimally developed character structures found in borderline schizophrenics.[9] If Polanski's horror films explore the personality dynamics of disturbed individuals modeled on this type, his modernist films further elaborate on schizoid structures by means of grotesque subject matter, illogical narrative patterns, exaggerated histrionics, and bizarre settings.

Such features dramatize a state of estrangement in which neither one's own character nor the world around one seems to offer any possibility for integrity and personal fulfillment. Perceiving a gaping emptiness as the essence of existence, absurdist art cannot comprehend the relatedness that could lead to love. In its place, it substitutes power. "When there is nothing left," says the hero of Mrozek's *Tango*, "and even revolt has become impossible, what can we then bring into being out of nothingness? . . . Only power! Only power can be created out of nothingness. It exists, even if nothing else exists."[10] In a similar spirit, Polanski's absurdist films are obsessed with shifting power relationships. In *Mammals*, two men quarrel over who will pull the other in their sleigh. In *Knife in the Water* the student and the husband continually jockey for supremacy by competing at various sorts of games.

In these films the strategy of gameplaying leads to an adversarial relationship between director and spectator much like that defined by Jerzy Growtowski. In the absurdist vision of meaninglessness, art itself is reduced to a game between the creator and the audience. To show off his superior "gamesmanship," Polanski repeatedly confronts us with surprising alternatives to the conventional patterns we anticipate, alternatives that undermine our expectations of meaningful narrative progression. In *Cul-de-Sac*, Albert lies dying in a car stolen from the Popular School of Motoring ("Prop'r Felix Bee") while the tide rises around him, wailing inconsequentially, "I've got a problem here!" And in *What?* Alex turns unexpectedly savage toward Nancy during their "game" of policeman and errant citizen. Such abrupt changes in tone are important to Polanski's purpose. Of *Cul-de-Sac*, the director has said, "If you look at this film very carefully, you will realize that almost every action, almost every word of dialogue is contrary to the expected."[11] A sense of the absurd underlies such strategies, for as Eugene Ionesco has said, "a living work of art is one that first of all surprises its own author, escapes from him and throws author and public into disarray, putting them in some way at variance with each other. Otherwise, creative work would be pointless, for why give a message that has already been given."[12]

The self-reflexive burlesque and parody often found in absurdist works comment ironically on the claim of art to fill the void at the center of existence. In a similar spirit, Polanski's modernist films are filled with mannered allusions to cinema and the other arts that undercut his role as a purveyor of eternal verities. Both *The Fat and the Lean* and *What?* can be read as cynical comments on art's pretensions to capture a transcendent truth. The surname of *Repulsion's* Carol Ledoux is a homage to the director of the Belgian Film Archives.[13] The master and slave in *The Fat and the Lean* are a grotesque version of Laurel and Hardy. The dance per-

formed by the tramps at the opening of *Two Men and a Wardrobe* recalls
Chaplin. Generic parody, an important generating principle in all of the
modernist films, serves similar purposes: *Knife in the Water* plays on the
narrative patterns of the socialist realist school; *Cul-de-Sac* is a self-conscious variation of the gangster-on-the-run and popular-romance formulas;
What? casts itself in the form of a pornographic parody of an *Alice-in-Wonderland* fantasy.

The self-reflexive aspect of Polanski's films is most dramatically an-
nounced by his own presence as an actor in many of them. His role as a
performer invariably carries overtones of self-mockery. In *Two Men and a
Wardrobe*, a young delinquent, played by the director himself, strikes out
at the screen; and in *Chinatown*, the audience, placed by Polanski's camera in the position of the protagonist, has its nose sliced by a hoodlum,
again played by the director. In *Two Men and a Wardrobe, Chinatown*,
and *What?* Polanski plays sadistic thugs; in *The Fat and the Lean* and
Dance of the Vampires, pathetically timid servants. In *When Angels Fall*
he becomes an old woman; in *The Tenant*, a transvestite. To watch him in
such roles is to identify him with the fantastic and the perverse, reminding
us that his other role behind the camera admits to similar interpretation.

For Polanski, all art expresses perverse desires, and this belief has gradually taken on greater psychological sophistication as he has absorbed the
themes and techniques of the surrealist movement. Unlike the nihilistic
absurdist sensibility, surrealism accepts one truth absolutely, the truth of
the unconscious mind; and this belief creates a positive base around which
Polanski has gradually erected a coherent and powerful aesthetic structure. The surrealists find the unconscious in dreams, which they use as a
model for their own art. "The theater will never find itself again—i.e. constitute a means of true illusion—except by furnishing the spectator with
the truthful precipitates of dreams," writes Artaud, "in which his taste for
crime, his erotic obsessions, his savagery, his chimeras, his utopian sense
of life and matter, even his cannibalism, pour out, on a level not counter-
feit and illusory, but interior."[14]

The surrealists have expressed their belief in dreams and the unconscious by creating new techniques of storytelling and imagery. In contrast
to the logically developed narrative structures of traditional art, surrealism
poses the alternative of automatic writing, which, like dreams, aims to
unlock the patterns and preoccupations of the unconscious mind. Polanski
has used similar free associative methods in his own scriptwriting. "I pre-
fer to write the script directly," he has said, "first loose scenes, putting
them together afterward."[15] And he describes *Cul-de-Sac* as "a script
which never had any line. How can I explain?—we didn't know what we
were going to do, we didn't have any theme. We just decided we wanted
to write what we feel, what we like."[16]

The surrealist technique of free association comes into play not only in the construction of narratives but also in the depiction of visual imagery, where again the haphazard and the eccentric are privileged. In his *History of Surrealism*, Maurice Nadeau defines a surrealist object as "any *alienated* object, used for purposes different from those for which it was intended, or whose purpose is unknown."[17] Polanski likes to focus on such "alienated" objects. In *Two Men and a Wardrobe*, a fish shot from above as it lies on a mirror reflecting the sky briefly appears to float in the air. And in *Cul-de-Sac* several octopuslike legs (wilted rhubarb?) dangle over the refrigerator door.

The surrealists' belief in the unconscious ultimately provides Polanski with a means of establishing a powerful and dynamic bond between himself and his audience, a bond built around the issue of sexuality. Psychoanalysis understands unconscious conflicts as primarily sexual, and while Polanski's early shorts do not focus on this issue, in all of his later work, as many critics have noted, sexuality plays a major role. In 1969, for instance, Colin McArthur pointed out that "*Knife in the Water* is a study in sexual rivalry, *Repulsion* of sexual disgust, and *Cul-de-Sac* of sexual humiliation. *Rosemary's Baby* (1968) teases the audience with the possibility that it is a study of sexual hysteria."[18] For Polanski, sexuality has become the primary mode by which the rituals of power, which have obsessed him from the beginning of his career, are enacted.

The struggle for power thus becomes a struggle for male dominance. In Polanski's world, women are typically either the hapless victims of male exploitations, as in *What?*, or, conversely, cold creatures who use their sexual charms to humiliate and abuse men, as in *Knife in the Water* and *Cul-de-Sac*. In the latter case, sexual role reversals expressed in styles of dress echo the humiliation such women inflict on their men. Thus, in *Knife in the Water*, when the wife and the young boy make love, she appears more masculine than he; and in *Cul-de-Sac* Teresa's mannish attire is complemented by the frilly nightgown and lipstick she forces her husband to wear. Such examples depict a world in which gender role defines gender rank.

The motif of sexual rivalry in Polanski's cinema has often been analyzed biographically.[19] But whatever the connection with the director's personal attitudes, experiences, or influences, the topic of sexuality is a natural extension of his surrealist interest in unconscious conflicts, and it provides a rich source of material by means of which he has been able to expand the thematic and technical scope of his art. Through sexuality, he explores the issues of domination and exploitation raised by the absurdist shorts in new, intense, and complex ways.

The sexually driven characters in Polanski's films range from Andrzej in *Knife in the Water* to Tess Durbyfield. But the role sexuality plays in his films is far more complex than the mere depiction of sexual case studies. The sexuality of the audience itself—and of the artist who is speaking to it—begins to concern him more and more as his work matures. Polanski examines the way in which his and our delight in pictures and stories can be seen as displaced sexual desire. The films insistently question the spectators to whom they are addressed, not only about what we are watching but also about why we are watching it. To this end, they increasingly confront us, in true surrealistic spirit, with the unconscious underpinnings of our own pleasure. This orientation is consonant with Polanski's often hostile attitude toward his audience both on and off the screen, for he believes that we do not understand the dynamics of our own responses. "I'm not interested in what the audience thinks," he told an interviewer, "because the audience is usually wrong."[20] What James Leach has called Polanski's "Cinema of Cruelty" is ultimately a cruelty aimed at the spectator, an aggressive strategy designed to unmask the prurient motives underlying our enjoyment of his art.[21]

To watch films, for Polanski, is to indulge in voyeurism. His audiences are repeatedly reminded of this by his use of peepholes and the connections he makes between looking and perverse sexual excitement. In *Knife in the Water*, for example, a young boy's glance is drawn to a woman undressing as a fly buzzes in the background; and in *What?* Joseph Noblart, owner of the villa in which the heroine finds herself stranded, becomes apoplectic as he gazes up between her legs. In this scene, too, a fly buzzes annoyingly, as though sexual desire were a disturbing irritation the characters would like to ignore or suppress. The voyeuristic pleasure the camera takes during *Cul-de-Sac* in observing Teresa dress George in her nightgown and deck him out in her makeup—in close-up—is wittily called into question when another spectator, Richard, observes their behavior from a more detached distance.

Though surrealism is committed to reproducing the perversity of unconscious thought processes, it often represents such imagery in an impersonally "realistic" manner. In his "First Manifesto of Surrealism," André Breton envisioned "the future resolution of these two states, dream and reality, which are seemingly so contradictory, into a kind of absolute reality, a surreality, if one may so speak."[22]

Such a formulation assumes that ordinary "reality" lies outside the mind, in the sphere of environmental and social phenomena. The so-called realist movement that flourished at the end of the nineteenth century deployed rationalistic ideals about nature and society as absolute truths. In our own time the political ends served by such reified conceptions of reality are explicitly acknowledged in the strictures of socialist realism, which applaud "working class nobility, strength, and victory."[23] Surrealists, by contrast, are reluctant to adopt such models as objective records of the world, regarding them as potentially projections of unconscious psychological and cultural preconceptions. Dali's theory of paranoia criticism provided an explicit model for this ambivalent preoccupation with realism. "Paranoia makes use of the external world to impose the obsessive notion with the disturbing particularly of making valid the reality of this notion for others. The reality of the external world serves as an illustration and a proof, and is put in the service of the reality of our mind."[24]

What this attitude means in terms of filmmaking is that the camera's ability to record the external world is no longer accepted unquestioningly. Hence, the process of recording becomes an exercise in stylization, reflecting the director's "obsession contradicted by irony" toward her or his visual and narrative materials. "The more I tell myself unbelievable stories," Polanski has explained, "the more conscious I am that I must render them in a realistic manner."[25] This concern, and its connection with surrealistic notions about paranoia, is explicitly suggested by one of the characters in *What?*, who comments, "I feel that there's some sort of intricate plot being hatched. Cunningly. Though I'm not sure if it's happening within me or outside."

For Polanski, reality is invariably problematic. Though he has often commented at length about his passion for realism,[26] he always presents this reality as somewhat askew. "What I like," he once said, "is an extremely realistic scene in which there is something that does not fit with the real."[27] That he owes a debt to surrealism for such a taste is suggested by his enthusiasm for Buñuel. "What I like most about [Buñuel's] films," he has said, "is that they are so *queer*."[28] This slightly jarring note reminds the audience that reality is not entirely to be trusted. In *Knife in the Water*, a young boy looks at a sailboat's mast first with one eye, then with the other. As his perspective shifts, we watch the image jump: a "realistic" depiction dramatically altered by a seemingly minute shift in the point of view from which it is perceived. Polanski's meticulously "objective" portrayal thus creates ambiguities through which reality itself becomes subjective and relative. "Among all the movies I have seen," the director has recalled, "I like *Citizen Kane* most, not only for the way it's done but for what it says. It says you never know the real truth about anyone."[29]

Polanski's commitment to realistic detail comes as a result of his conviction that "the only way to seduce people into believing you—whether they want to or not—is to take painstaking care with the details of your film, to make it accurate."[30] For this reason his style, like that of many of the surrealists, communicates an extraordinary tautness: the most outrageous violence and perversity are sheathed in a stylistic carapace of meticulous, hard-edged precision. "For me a film has to have a definite dramatic and visual shape," he has said, "as opposed to the rather flimsy shape that a lot of films were being given by the *Nouvelle Vague*, for example, which happened in more or less the same period. It has to be something finished, like a sculpture, almost something you can touch, that you can roll on the floor."[31] His films thus lack the improvisatory joie de vivre that tempers the apocalyptic sensibilities of a director like Jean-Luc Godard.

The director's penchant for presenting fantastic material in an ambiguously realistic manner is reflected in his lighting techniques. Like surrealist paintings, Polanski's films render their uncanny subjects with a studied, meticulous clarity, which he achieves by photographing his scenes at dawn or early evening, when diffuse light etches all objects with an eerie distinctness. "I like the atmosphere of morning and evening," he has explained. "I don't think there's a more beautiful hour then [sic] when the sun goes down and the light goes blue and the yellow light on the street goes shiny."[32] The portentous shot of the boats as they first appear in the harbor in Knife in the Water, seen from the point of view of the three main characters as they pull up in a car, and the haunting episode in which the Mexican boy on the horse talks to Jake Gittes in the rocky Los Angeles riverbed in Chinatown are memorable examples of this too-perfect depiction of the real world.

A closely related impulse leads Polanski to mimic the effect of real time and real space through the use of long takes and deep-focus photography. He believes that "if you don't need to cut it, there is no reason to cut."[33] In Cul-de-Sac, for instance, the scene in which George confesses his love for Teresa to Richard on the beach outside their castle is photographed in a continuous long take of eight and a half minutes, at the end of which a plane files overhead. To mount such a scene, of course, is an awesomely difficult task; and part of its force depends on the ambiguous relationship between its "realistic" view of the action and our lurking sense that this action is not "natural," but has been carefully orchestrated by a controlling consciousness to achieve precisely this effect. "It would have been easier, of course, to cut to the plane," Polanski has remarked of the shot. "But easy is not a reason: impossible is a reason."[34]

Deep-focus photography creates a similarly ambiguous realism. "You can increase the tension by having [many] things happen within the one second, or one and a half feet of film, of [a single] insert," the filmmaker has said.[35] The striking wide-angle three-shots in Knife in the Water show the characters unnaturally separated from one another while trapped in the same image. Scrupulously composed against the isolated lake setting, such shots present the world as an austere and alienating emotional hothouse filled with inescapable tensions. Similarly, in Two Men and a Wardrobe we often view the artless protagonists posed against a background or foreground of human depravity: all are ineluctably part of the same horrific universe. The tensions among many points of view often lead to irrational violence, motivated by unconscious drives that the characters can neither understand nor control. Thus, by the very ambiguity it creates, Polanski's use of the realist aesthetic allows the characters to read their surroundings subjectively, projecting their own unconscious obsessions onto the environment and acting them out.

Polanski's realism creates an atmosphere filled with sinister emotional resonances not only among his characters but also in his spectators. To Polanski, such a creation of atmosphere plays on the ambiguous correspondences between human emotion and the inanimate world. "Above everything else, cinema is atmosphere," he has said. "If you show a landscape, for instance, there will be very little atmosphere in it. But if you show the landscape and you hear a fly buzzing, immediately the atmosphere will heighten. Everything in a landscape can affect our emotional state."[36] His much-commented-on hyperesthetic use of sound—dripping faucets, ticking clocks, buzzing flies, shrieking gulls—defines an emotionally heightened reality. He likes an atmosphere that is "a little false, artificial, very studio, very 'cinema' . . . a world created anew."[37]

The "world created anew" in Polanski's films is thus a world in which the chaotic forces of the unconscious are unleashed in an absurd universe from which all of the traditional notions of meaning and value have vanished. The director implicates his audience in this world by insidiously undermining traditionally pious assumptions about ourselves and our environment. Underlying principles of significance and truth, Polanski finds unexamined needs for power and sexual release, which are expressed in the voyeuristic desire to watch and the paranoid fear of being watched. As his work has matured, Polanski has been increasingly drawn to the forms of conventional realism. Yet his modernist preoccupations are further developed when he brings them to bear on conventional narrative patterns, which have specific cultural associations for their audiences. But first the director had to develop his own personal style, and this the modernist aesthetic was well suited to encourage.

Absurdist Abstractions: The Shorts

Polanski has spoken of "a certain form that I believe proper to the short film. Strict, without dialogue."[38] Such an approach means that his actors must communicate through pantomime, which, especially when broadly exaggerated, produces an effect that is far from naturalistic. The artificiality thereby created is complemented by Krzysztof Komeda's music, which features simple themes orchestrated in eccentric ways, as well as by the films' crisply austere settings. True to the absurdist spirit, Polanski's short films all enact stylized, burlesqued power struggles in progressively briefer and more abstract modes. The cumulative effect is of fables, in which the moral becomes increasingly clarified as the form becomes increasingly spare. These films depict oppressive forces initially as a function of society and later as intrinsic to human nature itself.

The first of the shorts, *Two Men and a Wardrobe*, associates power with a ruthlessly conformist culture, so that the "moral" can be taken as direct social criticism. "*Two Men and a Wardrobe* is the only film I've made that 'meant' something," Polanski was to recall later. "It was about the intolerance of society toward somebody who was different."[39] This thesis is presented through a theme and variation structure. The film follows two men carrying a wardrobe as they try to gain access to various social institutions (a restaurant, a hotel, a streetcar), only to be rejected from each with increasing hostility. As the story progresses, images of violence grow more intense and the images of conformism become more abstract. After receiving a brutal beating from a gang of thugs, the two return to the sea across a beach on which a little boy is engaged in making hundreds of identical sand castles.

The plot thus deteriorates rather than develops. Though we last see the two men retreating back into the sea from which they initially emerged, they are worse off than they were at the beginning: not only have they been rudely disabused of their innocence in the town, but even the pristine beach has been encroached upon by neophyte purveyors of rigid and repetitive conformism.

Though its narrative variations and detailed mise-en-scène make this film the least abstract of Polanski's shorts, it is not naturalistic. A preternatural opening image in which the two men emerge from the sea immediately establishes an atmosphere of fantasy and fable. The two men perform a celebratory, clownlike dance and indulge in some beguiling pantomime to the accompaniment of Komeda's eccentric, folkish music, thereby giving their eccentricity a winsome cast.

Two Men and a Wardrobe pits these empathic protagonists against a hostile society, but it is already clear that the problem is not with society per se but with human nature. Here, as in so many of the later films, the most idyllic natural settings are marred by images of human depravity. A man standing on a picturesque bridge overlooking a river, apparently to admire the view, puts his arm around another only to avail himself of the opportunity to steal the latter's wallet out of his back pocket. A little later in the woods, we watch as one man batters in the head of another with a rock. "The struggle is with reality, more than with society," Polanski has said of the film. "The individual can live in the jungle or be a hermit, so that there's no society around him. The interest in the individual is always against society, and the interest of society is always against the individual."[40]

In Polanski's films, the interest of the spectator may also be against the interest of the director, who may reveal himself to be as sadistic and depraved as the society he depicts. *Two Men and a Wardrobe* suggests such a dynamic in a scene involving the director as an actor. As the two men are beginning to leave the town, they come upon a troupe of young people in an outdoor theater, some sitting on a stage, others in the audience, amusing themselves by throwing rocks at a kitten. Catching sight of a pretty girl, one of the group decides to frighten her by dangling the now-dead kitten in her face. But she catches sight of the mischiefmaker in the mirror of the wardrobe, which the two protagonists are still faithfully carrying about, and this enables her to foil their plot. Disappointed in his scheme, the chief plotter instructs one of his minions to give the two men a beating. The "hit man," played by the director, aims his first blow directly at the camera. This aggressive attack on his audience, and the implied statement behind it about the perversely punitive pleasure provided by cinema and the theater, establishes a motif that Polanski will vary and develop with extraordinary richness as his work matures.

Polanski was not to make such a directly aggressive statement to his audience again, however, until later in his career. In the next absurdist short, *The Fat and the Lean*, the spectator becomes a character. Like the fat, sloppy master who requires his shabby servant (played by Polanski the actor) to entertain him and minister to his needs, we demand diversion from Polanski the filmmaker. When the servant tries to escape from his constricting environment to the fairy-tale city that hovers on the horizon, his master presents him with a goat, which, in turn, threatens to lead the young man astray. The master then chains it to his servant's ankle, thereby constricting the latter's movements still further. The more the servant is oppressed, however, the more eager he is to please his "audience." We last see him frantically making an endless number of identical paper flowers, which he carefully plants, row after row, in the soil around the ancient, decaying chateau.

In the context of *Two Men and a Wardrobe*, this final image suggests a false conformity to acceptable values in a society that denies freedom. Unlike the earlier film, however, the freedom that is here denied is artistic. "I didn't give them a piano to carry," Polanski has said of *Two Men and a Wardrobe*, "because that would have implied a specific difference that set them apart, like art."[41] In *The Fat and the Lean*, he appears to have taken up this other option by making his servant not only an accomplished pantomimist and dancer but also a musician and a creator of images. Such a portrait of the artist as servant implies that constraint spurs creative energy and that the artist is a willing slave to the domineering standards imposed by the authority of the society in which she or he lives. Though this film was made in France, Polanski was soon to return to Poland to make *Knife in the Water*, and it is tempting to see the audience here as the Soviet censors, who were accustomed to making Polish directors jump through hoops for the betterment of the state. Artistic constraints need not be part of an officious government policy, however; they can just as easily operate through the marketplace, as happens in Western cultures. The possibility of such alternative interpretations is suggested by the setting of the film, a crumbling estate, and by the master-servant relationship, both of which connote an aristocratic framework.

The Fat and the Lean derives still other motifs from the tradition of Hollywood filmmaking—its artist-hero recalls Chaplin and its coupling of a fat master and a thin servant caricatures Laurel and Hardy. In uncomfortable ways, such devices suggest that popular film artists enact their psychic perversions to entertain a passive, pampered audience ever more gluttonous about having its slightest emotional whims indulged. This self-reflexive dimension is emphasized in the final sequence, when the servant's redoubled efforts to please are depicted in fast-motion, thereby recalling the slapstick antics of silent film comedies.

This device also suggests the built-in compulsion in modern culture to create faster and faster simply in order to feel that one is keeping up. As Raymond Durgnat has pointed out, Polanski's film can be seen as a parable of modern technological society, in which "man is ostensibly given freedom so that he will enthusiastically overfulfill the duties which make him a slave, and banish even dreams of escape (which, ironically, is from this rural arcady to our office-block world)."[42]

As in other Polanski films, the cumulative impression is of an entropic system in which energy is increasingly wasted as the quality of life deteriorates. This theme is repeated in even more abstract terms in *Mammals*. Stark contrasts of black and white dominate the visuals, which focus on snow-covered fields over which two tramps, seen primarily in distancing long-shots, take turns pulling each other in a sledge. The affection between the two is reminiscent of *Two Men and a Wardrobe* and is again emphasized by mannered, clownish performances. But the sadomasochistic undertones of the relationship here dominate the portrayal as each man feigns evermore serious disabilities in order to avoid pulling the other. The end result of their squabbling is that the sled is stolen from them, at which point they resume their game of privilege-through-weakness by offering each other piggyback rides. Characteristically, by the end they are worse off than they are at the beginning, though they have learned nothing from their experience.

The portrait, with all its charm, is a devastating one. Pathetic in their affections, which are at bottom mere dependencies, the two tramps wallow in petty pastimes—knitting, plucking a chicken—which are only minimally constructive. And they soon abandon them in the interests of ill-conceived power games that deprive both of them of the little headway they had established at the outset. Such a contemptuous view of human nature, while it is closely related to that of other modernist artists such as

Beckett, shapes all of Polanski's early work, and he was not to modify it seriously until he reexamined the whole tradition in *Tess*.

The Subversion of Socialist Realism: *Knife in the Water*

"This game's not just so many sticks," someone announces at one point in *Knife in the Water*. "It's a whole system." In the film as a whole, the "system" of power relationships is expressed through games, actual and psychological. In this, his first feature, made from a script he had coauthored with another aspiring Polish director, Jerzy Skolimowski, sexuality entered Polanski's cinematic world, and the games of power became more complicated.

In contrast to the early shorts, *Knife in the Water* etched its theme on a naturalistic surface, thereby ostensibly following the strictures of socialist realism. Everything here is plausible; the people are ordinary. The story concerns Andrzej, a successful sports journalist, and his wife, Krystyna, who pick up a young hitchhiker and take him with them on an overnight sailing expedition. Polanski was uncomfortable with the naturalistic tone he had adopted, wondering later "if this film is not slightly too realistic for me." He compensated by portraying the action in a highly stylized manner. Noticeably slow pacing, elegantly posed deep-focus compositions shot from unexpected angles, heightened sound, Krzyzstof Komeda's languid jazz score, and unnatural, ominous silences establish a mood based on "ambiguity, on little ironies, on a kind of cynicism in halftones."[43]

Both the stylization and the irony made *Knife in the Water* unpopular with Soviet-bloc critics, despite its ostensibly doctrinaire social message.[44] Though Polanski had criticized decadent Western materialism by focusing on the contrasting "economic positions" of the two men, he had not countered his indictment with any positive socialist values to provide a constructive example.[45] And even a Western commentator noticed that it had "no propaganda value whatever."[46] Based on the evidence Polanski had provided, life in Communist Poland presented a grim picture, without heroes and without progress. The protagonist's Peugeot and his sailboat, which he calls *Christine*, an Anglicized version of his wife's name, epitomize Western consumerism. His rivalry with the boy caricatures capitalist competition. Yet the young boy himself, who could have represented more positive values, is no different. "You're not one bit better than he is," the woman tells the youth near the end of the film. "And you'd really like to be the way he is now." The boy's knife, the coiled rope forming a halo around his head while he is lying on the deck, and his "walking on the water" all present a jaded comment on his presumed position as the virile Messiah of the new Poland. Thus, rather than enacting the ideal of "working class nobility, strength, and victory" posited by Soviet socialist realism, Polanski's film exposes universal decadence and venality. In view of this overriding cynicism, it was hardly surprising that Gomulka denounced the film in 1964.

With its emphasis on social renewal, the spirit of socialist realism grows out of the more universal patterns of comedy, and Polanski's emphasis on sexuality in *Knife in the Water* plays in particular on the conventions of romantic comedy. In keeping with the absurdist technique of upsetting audience expectations, *Knife in the Water* reverses the traditional comic pattern, which, according to a classic formulation offered by Northrop Frye, centers on a young man who wins the love of a young woman by triumphing over an older, paternal figure. In the process, a new, healthier society is also born.[47] Polanski portrays a similar conflict, but resolves it by affirming not the regeneration of the social order but the anguish of alienation.

The struggle of youth versus age, from this perspective, dissolves into meaningless caricature. The boy, at one point, ties his handkerchief around his neck as a bib; his "parents" smile indulgently as he paddles the boat around in circles. He solemnly recites a poem to Krystyna about a child's love for his mother. And finally, when his sexuality triumphs, he encounters oedipal taboos: he is "castrated" by the father figure (his knife is thrown overboard), and he makes love to the mother. Such an incestuous and emasculating outcome represents a grotesque inversion of the spirit of sexual and social renewal that lies at the heart both of traditional comedy and of the socialist realist ideal.[48]

The real subject of *Knife in the Water* is not regeneration, but anomie, as symbolized in the film's title image. The boy, who represents the hope for future change, flourishes a knife. "You need a knife like that," he says, "especially in a forest. It's useless on water, but in a forest, where you have to force your way through the thicket. . . . " Nonetheless, he takes the knife on the lake, where his ideal of purposeful action becomes meaningless. Any impulse toward regeneration is thereby dissolved in a primal image of existential nothingness, which renders the ideals of social progress and psychological development absurd. The boy finally loses his knife to this vast and undifferentiated watery environment, just as his will is absorbed into the void of a meaningless existence, symbolized by his pointless adventures. He has learned nothing, achieved nothing; it has all been a waste of time.

This is the absurdist response to the easy optimism purveyed by much socialist realism. But the film contains another, more pervasive dimension, which Polanski was to develop with greater sophistication in subsequent work. By focusing on Andrzej, the film's protagonist, it speaks to political questions in terms of some of their most intimate manifestations, which are sexual.[49] At this level *Knife in the Water* becomes a fable not of absurdist anomie but of the psychological dynamics at the root of political power and oppression.

These dynamics are symbolized by games. The initial sequence between the couple themselves, which lasts only a little over six minutes, defines the power relationships in the film and the kinds of games that express them. Initially the camera's position favors Andrzej, identifying him as the protagonist. But his agitated behavior and irritated expression along with the fleeting shadows that repeatedly fall across his features upset our empathy with him by creating an alienating sense of friction and unrest. Krystyna, sexual and distant in a low-necked sweater and impish glasses, represents his frustrated desire: though her appearance seduces him, emotionally she is unavailable. Even the desperately impassioned kiss he plants on the back of her neck has no effect. Unable to reach her, he can only reassert his impotence by cajoling and criticizing, repeatedly provoking her capacity for anger and active rejection. If he cannot have her love, he can, at least, control her. In this game, she acquiesces, her passivity countering her husband's bravado in their battle for dominance. As she leaves the car, ostensibly in deference to his superior competence at the wheel, the voice on the radio commands: "Arms up. And arms to the side," mocking the victory Andrzej has attained; for she has granted him only a similarly puppetlike obeisance.

Yet she also has desires, which surface as she smiles at the young hitchhiker. Her husband can now hope to win the match by asserting his superiority over the boy, thereby proving his own worthiness as an object of her lust. Krystyna, however, outwits him even here by seducing the boy herself. At the same time, she neatly checkmates her husband's efforts to establish his dominance by offering him the choice of two alternatives, both of which constitute tacit admissions of his weakness: either he is a cuckold or a killer.

For the most part, the camera views this struggle impartially, adjusting its position to the center of the windshield after the initial shot, in which Andrzej is favored. It also draws closer to the couple as the stakes of the game become clearer, adopting more intimate, almost claustrophobic perspectives—even vaguely menacing ones—that define our own ambivalence about witnessing the perverse underpinnings of their "ordinary" behavior. By picking up the youth, Andrzej hopes to engage in an unfamiliar activity, which could enliven their stagnant relationship and call into question his wife's smug complacency. As Krystyna watches her husband go out to talk to the boy, the camera moves away from her point of view to adopt that of the newcomer. Its motion—the first it has made in the film—foreshadows the newly dynamic interplay his presence will introduce. The appearance of the boy throws Krystyna off balance: she moves closer to her husband, inclining her body toward his for the first time. If Krystyna feels threatened, however, so does her husband. After Andrzej pushes the youth into the back seat, the compositions privilege Krystyna's perspective, shooting the two men from her side of the car, for

from this point on she assumes an observing role akin to that of the
spectator.

After the initial sequence, the emphasis shifts from Andrzej's struggle
with his wife to his struggle with the boy, who mirrors himself. Again, the
stake is power, which is seen as potency. It is enacted through games: the
game of pick-up-sticks, the contest to blow up the mattresses, the knife-
throwing contest, and the game in which the knife is manipulated
between the fingers of the participants. Ostensibly, these are harmless
diversions, but they mask a real and deadly rivalry for the possession of
the woman. "You want to go on with the game?" the youth inquires of
Andrzej when the older man invites him on the sailing expedition, at
which Andrzej laughs—though at this point no "games" have yet been
played.

As Sybil March has noted, the prize that will go to the winner of this
contest is to be Krystyna.[50] The boy's sexual enthrallment by her is as complete as that of his elder. Krystyna's body, scantily clad in a bikini, is prominently exhibited, and she hums a sirenish song at one point, which she
later sings to the boy. Its words describe a dying love affair—perhaps the
story of her own marriage. These oblique hints do not go unheeded. A
low-angle, deep-focus shot early in the film observes the boy in the distance watching Krystyna's feet as she takes her shoes off close to the camera. Later, she will offer him her slipper. In the evening the boy catches
sight of her as she undresses, and just before she finally seduces him he
sees her nude again.

Though the prize is finally an empty one, snatched away as soon as it is
offered, the game between the two men is ruthlessly played. The weapons
Andrzej brings are wealth and experience: he continually flaunts his pos-
sessions and his knowledgeability before the younger man. These, however, are only substitutes for his more fundamental lack of physical vitality,
which the boy's presence accentuates. Andrzej's deteriorating body cannot
hope to match the boy's strength and agility. Through his profession as a
sportswriter, the older man has already defined his role as that of an im-
potent voyeur in the realm of contests involving physical prowess. As Andrzej loses strength, the boy gains it. When left alone in the older man's
boat early in the film, the youth loses control of it and finds himself en-
meshed in ropes as in a spider's web. Later, after first glimpsing Krystyna's
nude body, however, he kills the fly whose buzzing has been distracting
him. The following morning, Andrzej comes on deck to witness the
youth's black-clad figure crouched atop the mast with ropes emanating
around it, looking itself like a gigantic and deadly spider.

The struggle ends in violence, an assertion of power in its rawest physical form. This outcome represents a further regression of Andrzej, since
he experiences it in part as a fragmentation of his double's body. When the
journalist wakens in the morning alone and suspects that the boy is dally-

Andrzej and the young hitchhiker compete for Krystyna's attention in Knife in the
Water. *Courtesy of the Film Stills Archive, The Museum of Modern Art, New York.*

ing with his wife, his first impulse is not to confront his opponent directly
but to steal the young man's knife, a symbol of his potency. After the boy
has disappeared, Andrzej desperately attempts to dispose of the youth's
belongings, not only to destroy the evidence of his own wrongdoing but
also out of a befuddled sense that to destroy his rival's accoutrements—his
food and his clothing—is tantamount to destroying the boy's threatening
potency. He is, however, unable even to accomplish this diminished and
displaced assertion of dominance, being reduced, ultimately, to a humili-
ating scuffle with Krystyna herself, who responds contemptuously to this
gross assertion of mastery based on the superior strength of the male body
by calling him a clown.

Like many of Polanski's protagonists, Andrzej is ultimately reduced to an almost catatonic immobility. A frustrated desire that was originally erotic has been converted into one charged with hostility, so that he wishes only to destroy the object of his lust by dominating and controlling her. Failing this, he vents his rage against himself, first through a surrogate, then more directly, by tacitly acquiescing to his wife's victory over him.

His defeat, however, inspires little empathy, for Polanski's cold stylization keeps the audience at a distance, presenting the action itself as a carefully orchestrated game. Movement and dialogue are often portrayed in artificially dancelike counterpoint. As the boy reflects on the meaning of his knife, for instance, he is shown in close-up; but as he turns to address his companions, he moves his body slightly so that they too are "conveniently" revealed to the camera's gaze. And later, a striking overhead shot reveals the trio of characters elegantly arranged on the deck like players on a chessboard.

If all of the characters are objectified in this way, however, Krystyna suffers most. She is victorious, but she is absolutely empty. In *Knife in the Water* the woman is seen almost exclusively in terms of a male perspective: as an object of lust. In contrast to the men, she has no visible interests. As an object, she is idolized; as a person, ignored. The protracted physical struggle between youth and age enacted by the two men is not permitted her; for her body is seen as potent primarily as a symbol of desire rather than as an agent of her own will. She understands her role as the prize of the competition between the men as a natural extension of her position as one of her husband's accoutrements, like his boat and his car. Her frolicking with the inflated crocodile dramatizes the fact that she herself only exists to be a plaything for her husband. She accepts this position also, reacting with outrage only when Andrzej physically attacks her. She lacks an autonomous presence because the world Polanski creates allows her no identity.

That Krystyna's smug feminine conceit might mask a more complicated sexual dynamic in which women suffer more consequential victimization than men was not to become an issue in Polanski's work until the popular horror films. His other modernist films, *Cul-de-Sac* and *What?*, did not demand such connections between social and psychological phenomena; and the view of sexual politics they present is much the same as the one-sided presentation in *Knife in the Water*.

Fantasies of Escape: *Cul-de-Sac*

Of all Polanski's features, the most personal are *Cul-de-Sac* and *What?* Both were original screenplays coauthored by the director and his long-time friend French writer-publicist Gerard Brach, and both were produced under conditions of great freedom. The screenplay for the former project was composed in 1963–64, after the international recognition garnered by *Knife in the Water* had encouraged the director to move to Paris. There he began his long association with Brach, with whom he was to coauthor *Cul-de-Sac, Repulsion, The Fearless Vampire Killers, What?*, and *The Tenant.* Throughout their partnership, Brach appears to have done the actual writing, casting the pair's ideas into specific dialogue. "We talk and then he writes it and then I come back into the room, and he reads it, and we change it," Polanski has explained.[51]

Once the script for *Cul-de-Sac* was completed, the two had difficulty obtaining financing for the project, so they set to work on a popular thriller, *Repulsion,* which another Polish expatriate, Gene Gutowski, arranged for Filmways to produce in England. The success of *Repulsion* encouraged Filmways to back *Cul-de-Sac.* Polanski's repeated claim that *Cul-de-Sac* is his best film has often been echoed by critics, though very little has actually been written about it. Ironically, *Repulsion* has been discussed far more fully. "*Cul-de-Sac* was the greatest disaster I've ever had in America," Polanski recalled in 1973 as he was finishing *What?*, which was destined to become an even more spectacular flop.[52]

The film's debt to absurdism is unmistakable. "I was certainly influenced by modern theater, by Beckett, by Ionesco and by Pinter also," the director has said of it. "By all this type of atmosphere."[53] The film's original title, *When Katelbach Comes,* recalls *Waiting for Godot.* And echoes of Pinter abound in the sexual hostility and in the relationship between the two gangsters, who are similar to the ones in *The Dumb Waiter.* In the absurdist spirit, *Cul-de-Sac* replaces traditional characters and story with caricatures and fragmented bits of burlesque that repeatedly call attention to the artifice behind artistic illusions. The director himself can be identified with the two subservient gangsters by virtue of the association of the name of their employer, Katelbach, with that of Andre Katelbach, the actor who played the role of an equally inhumane master to Polanski's timid servant in *The Fat and the Lean.*

Like *Knife in the Water, Cul-de-Sac* treats a situation in which a married couple's sexual tensions erupt into violence when an outsider intrudes on their world. Both films depict "somebody coming into somebody else's life, where relations and the situation are already set," as the director has described it.[54] But the exercise is more abstract than in the earlier film. It features a setting and histrionics calculated to bring out the bizarre. And its narrative is more fragmented. "We just sat down and decided to write whatever we wanted to, just what we wanted to see on the screen," Polanski was to say of it, "completely disconnected things, just feelings and characters."[55]

As the film's title implies, the audience's expectations are here focused on collective fantasies of escape rather than on fantasies of social regeneration, as in *Knife in the Water.* Such fantasies are self-consciously invoked in the narrative through the incorporation of fragments from two different escape formulas well known to Western audiences: the gangster-on-the-run genre and the romantic melodrama.

In the American gangster-on-the-run formula, the protagonists, played by stars like Humphrey Bogart and James Cagney, often appear as rebellious, romantically alienated outsiders at odds with a dull, bourgeois world. As Robert Warshow expressed it in his essay "The Gangster as Tragic Hero," "the gangster's whole life is an effort to assert himself as an individual, to draw himself out of the crowd."[56] By creating such heroes, the genre typically offers "a way of gaining a perspective on society by creating a world and figures that are outside it."[57] But in *Cul-de-Sac* the gangsters, Richard and Albert, are far more conventional than the "family" they intrude on. Instead of seeing themselves as rebellious individualists, they seem content to remain cogs in a bureaucratic machine, timidly respectful of their boss Katelbach. Both dress conservatively and betray attitudes best described as prim: Richard considers George a "queer," and Albert's main concern is for his wife, Doris. The relationship between the two men themselves seems much more affectionately familiar than that of George and Teresa. Richard's hard-boiled code of ethics is mocked by his attachment to small pieties. He is extravagantly dismayed when George accidentally breaks Albert's glasses. "Real mean of you to smash his glasses. Just because Albie didn't go into the hospital," Richard snaps, ridiculously invoking the illogic that often accompanies blind moral fervor. "How could you?"

Later some quintessentially bourgeois guests arrive: the plump, nosy Fairweathers with their incorrigible son Horace; and the vapid, "trendy" couple Cecil and Jackie. The myopic self-satisfaction of this group makes them seem more threatening than the gangsters themselves, who are portrayed as possessing some sense of personal responsibility and moral integrity. Rather than try to appeal to them for help, as the formula would ordinarily dictate, George perfunctorily dismisses them, preferring to take his chances with the more old-fashioned mode of conventionality represented by Richard, who can at least be trusted not to seduce his wife or shoot guns off at random—as some of the guests do. Even George and Richard, however, cannot form a stable social tie, for the gangster is ultimately murdered by his "host." By this act, however, George and Teresa are not liberated, as the formula would have dictated, but instead radically traumatized and alienated from one another, the precarious fantasy that has held them together destroyed.

That fantasy belongs to George, who plays the role of the alienated rebel far more explicitly than do the outlaws. George's fantasy is based on the legend of Lindesfarne castle, where Sir Walter Scott wrote *Rob Roy* and where George now lives. "Don't know how to tell stories like that anymore," the castle's new owner confides to Richard. George himself has

Richard objects to George's transvestite attire in Cul-de-Sac. *Courtesy of* Cinema Journal.

escaped from a settled, prosperous life as a factory owner to undertake a dashing, bucolic existence with a beautiful young maiden in the castle, echoing a favorite romance plot involving a poor girl who falls in love with a rich, aristocratic man.[58] Yet the fairy-tale castle is, in George's own words, "impossible to seal in the winter . . . not practical . . . and then . . . draughts . . . peculiar."

But the central factor in George's fantasy is not the castle; it is love. His longing for romantic fulfillment, however, is destined to remain unsatisfied. "I worship her," he confesses to Richard on the beach after his wife, Teresa, has temporarily abandoned them so that she can swim nude in the ocean. Unlike a nineteenth-century heroine, Teresa regards sexuality as a casual pleasure, not as romance, and she is aggressive and indiscriminate in her quest to satisfy this craving. As Marian Fairweather bluntly puts it, she will "go to bed with anything in trousers." Like Krystyna in *Knife in the Water*, she uses her appearance to give her an advantage in sexual politics, and she is much more masculine than the Polish woman in Polanski's earlier film—not only in the way she dresses but in her behavior. At one point, she self-consciously burlesques the role of a male to complement the transvestite creature she has made of her husband. Later, briefly, she playfully adopts the persona of Scott himself. By such means she assumes the traditional role of creator and controller of sexual fantasies, not the object of them, though Geroge tries desperately to make her into such an object through his obsessive painting of her image. Like Krystyna, however, Teresa appears to have no autonomous will or interior life.

And like Krystyna, Teresa taunts her husband for not being more of a "man," a charge he invites by his appearance as well as his behavior. Next to his sleek, narcissistic wife, George looks pathetic. His baldness, his awkwardly shaped physique, and his unflattering clothes make him a fig-ure of contempt, and he masochistically exaggerates his ungainliness by his foolishly inept juggling and his meek transvestism. Critic Tom Milne rightly observes that "George is a man betrayed by his body."[59] Halfway through the film, Teresa and Richard almost bury him alive.

Finally, the roles are righted: Teresa, for the first time, wears a dress, a romantic one, reaching to the floor. And George, in properly masculine clothes, acts out a conventional male role by protecting his home and his woman through a dramatic act of violence. Ironically, the role he assumes is the one defined by the other, more contemporary fantasy of masculine potency represented by Richard, the man he kills: that of the alienated lawbreaker. "Villains . . . murderers . . . cowards . . .," George shouts wildly at Cecil, who has returned for his gun, "the whole pack of you against one man." At last, he breaks down entirely, plaintively calling the name of his first wife from a tremblingly fetal pose on a rock in the middle of the flooded causeway.

The pathos of his plight, however, is undercut by the coldly grotesque depiction of his character, which prevents us from empathizing with him. Donald Pleasance plays the role in a stylized and histrionic manner calcu-lated to alienate the audience, and Polanski's camera complements his performance through self-conscious devices that distance us from the ac-tion. George is shown at one point in an extreme wide-angle shot taken as if from a mirror as he is admiring his transvestite attire—a shot made even more alienating by its implicit suggestion that George and the spectator are mirror images of one another.

Other shots, taken through small peephole-like apertures, imply that spectators have perversely voyeuristic motives for observing the intimate activities of others' lives. The character most identified with this observing function is, ironically enough, Richard, who peers at the couple from the wine cellar and the chicken coop and watches them as they sleep together. Richard draws conventional conclusions about the nature of George's sex-uality after witnessing his strange garb on their initial encounter. The gangster's unsophisticated judgment that George is "a queer" leaves the audience with the uncomfortable choice of either judging and dismissing George's actions by conventional standards as Richard does, which seems overly naive, or taking pleasure in them as Teresa does, which seems perverse. This sense of emotional dislocation characterizes the film as a whole. Photographed in a starkly contrasting black-and-white style, *Cul-de-Sac* presents its nihilistic vision austerely. The irritating repetitiousness of Krzysztof Komeda's score suggests the meaningless, static nature of the action: nothing is going anywhere. Though the gangster-on-the-run formula contains elements of social satire, these are invoked in *Cul-de-Sac* not to criticize social practices but to illustrate the absurdity of the genre's traditional formulation of social norms. Similarly, the ridiculousness of George's romantic quest emerges more as a cynical comment on traditional formulas of romantic adventure than as a study of psychological trauma. Thus, both social conflict and sexual politics are finally irrelevant, for *Cul-de-Sac* attempts neither a comprehensive portrait of society nor a cogent vision of individual personality. To show us how little we can know outside our own interior world, it is self-consciously artificial, turning characters into stereotypes, plot and theme into playful parody. The protests of many reviewers that the film is pointless thus have a certain validity. "Of course it wasn't just a story," George protests at one point in defense of Scott's novel *Rob Roy.* To which Marian Fairweather replies with unconscious acuity, "But . . . but, yes. . . . They made a film of it."

The Politics of Art: *What?*

Polanski's involvement with modernist principles ultimately led him to make *What?*, a film that represented for his artistic development a far more definitive cul-de-sac than his earlier film of that title. Carlo Ponti, who produced it, took a hands-off attitude toward the project. "I had no interference at all," Polanski later recalled. "I did it with Ponti, and I must say, you have no problems with him. I saw him maybe twice during the production."[60] Yet, despite this freedom—or perhaps because of it— *What?* was also Polanski's least successful film, both commercially and critically. Though it garnered some praise in France, English-language critics, on the whole, found it "tiresome, needlessly spun-out, obvious, and heavy handed."[61]

As the most fragmented and stylized of Polanski's projects, *What?* offers virtually no character or narrative development. Its plot is cast in the form of a pornographic parody of *Alice in Wonderland:* Nancy, a naive but earnest young American girl, goes down an outdoor elevator instead of a rabbit hole, confronting European decadence in a series of Alice-like encounters with the sexually preoccupied denizens of a luxurious villa on the Italian Riviera belonging to Joseph Noblart, a wealthy patron of the arts. The "negation of history," which Lukács sees as the informing principle of modernism, operates in the film on both a personal and social level. At one point the heroine confesses to being troubled by a sense of déjà vu: her actions seem repetitive, but as they lead nowhere, it is hard to keep track of the specific content of any of them.

The film's idyllic setting and cheerful, sunny atmosphere make light of the nihilism and despair that inform it. It examines people without principles or purpose, who pass the time by copulating, eating gourmet food, and relishing the sound of crunching Ping-Pong balls. A similar sybaritic emptiness is expressed in the film's ambience. The setting blithely mixes Selig catcher's mitt and lip chairs with fine old Italian antiques, and the doings of the comic-book characters are depicted to the strains of Mozart and Bach in the background. Such juxtapositions reveal a world in which values have caved in on one another, in which meaning is subjective and shifting rather than absolute and permanent.

The conspicuous magnificence of the setting is appropriate, for *What?* is concerned with the nature and place of art in the contemporary world. In the absence of stable values, power becomes the only principle by which artistic norms may be established. Noblart's very name suggests the position of privilege that allows him the disinterested pleasure of aesthetic appreciation. In one episode, he is the absent center of a conflict over Géricault's *The Raft of the Medusa*. The painting has apparently been stolen for his collection at the request of his "half-witted" nephew Alex, one of the many hangers-on living in the villa, who hopes to ingratiate himself with Noblart by this scheme. Nancy's declaration that the painting is "a masterpiece" seems beside the point in this scenario of buying and selling, in which all parties concerned see the transaction solely as an enactment of economic power relationships. Art thus becomes merely another commodity.

Its value as a commodity lies in its ability to provide a substitute for direct erotic stimulation. In *What?* all forms of art are revealed as perverse displacements of sexual pleasure. The characters dress up and perform tableaux, the better to whip themselves into a state of sexual excitement. Often the playacting is violent, suggesting the need for extreme, sexualized manifestations of the master-slave pattern that is assumed to lie at the core of all human relationships. Alex, a self-proclaimed pimp, enacts his affection for Nancy by, among other things, prancing around his bedroom in a tiger skin begging her to whip him. Two other characters, Jimmy and Lollipop, copulate endlessly under a rug while Lollipop shouts, "Give!" at Jimmy and he responds, "Take!" Reason and emotion have here given way to an obsession with pure sensation; and art, as well as life, suffers the consequences.

Noblart himself has succumbed to this reductionism and has discovered that, in terms of sensation, art is wanting. "He'd rather eat an apple than look at an apple," someone says of him at one point. "Having spent his

The Raft of the Medusa *by Théodore Gericault (1818–19). Courtesy of the Louvre, Paris.*

whole life preferring the image to the object, recently he's found that he prefers the object to the image." The "object" he prefers above all others is the young American heroine's genitals. To contemplate this vision seems to him the culmination of erotic pleasure. On finally attaining his goal, he is moved to a fit of ecstasy that culminates in his death.

As the only major female character, Nancy goes through the film in various states of undress, only to find that her body has become a spectacle to be looked at and commented on by everyone. Like art, she exists as an object to be exhibited as a stimulant for the voyeurism of the males around her—and presumably the audience as well. "A brown nipple against a milky white breast is really something worth looking at," observes Alex, who, like most of the other male characters, fancies himself a connoisseur of the female form. As a purely physical presence, the only change Nancy undergoes lies in her progressive loss of clothing. Finally, she finds herself completely naked.

In the face of such reductionistic attitudes, Nancy's attempts to express a spiritual or intellectual presence—most conspicuously in her diary—are held up to public ridicule by the other guests in the villa. This audience reacts to Nancy as the audience of the film itself is encouraged to, for her attempts at seriousness are never allowed the slightest credibility. Dutifully writing her experiences down in a diary, she solemnly invests her absurd adventures with false significance. "A mad priest—shocking!" she writes. "WHAT'S THE CHURCH COMING TO?"

Her attempts to discover meaning in her experiences make her appear only slightly less absurd than Pietro, the hypocritical "mad priest," who represents another of Polanski's attacks on religion. Pietro condemns the behavior of the others by invoking anachronistic slogans while himself enjoying the largesse of the villa. "Don't be enticed by comfort and the easy life here," he warns Nancy. "Get away! There's decadence and decay everywhere here—these people can turn rocks to dust just by looking at them." In *What?*, however, comfort and the easy life are the only values that exist, and to denounce them in the name of a chimerical morality appears ludicrous.

The perversity that motivates artistic creation and appreciation in *What?* involves not only exhibitionistic display but also paranoid projection. Being observed, therefore, is not only pleasurable but also threatening. The characters constantly fear being spied on or overheard. Even the most innocent actions are monitored. "It'd be better to meet on the beach or up in the tower," Alex says to Nancy at one point. "Otherwise they'll be watching us like hawks." And a thoughtful gesture performed by Nancy when she thinks she is alone is greeted by a brief bit of handclapping.

Polanski's jaded perspective expresses itself not only in the world *in* the film, but also in the world *of* the film. *What?* was set in the villa of its producer, Carlo Ponti, whose extravagant and rarefied tastes are evident throughout in the lavish furnishings and works of art that form a backdrop to the action. In the character of Noblart, such privileged personages are seen as the patrons of artists. As Noblart's munificence makes Alex's "theatricals" possible, so does Ponti's patronage indulge Polanski. The character of Mosquito is played by the director himself, who has used the opportunity to comment ironically on his role as a creator of fantasy. (A similar self-reflexive relationship between the filmmaker and a creative "godfather" figure would be repeated in *Chinatown*, made the following year.)

Mosquito's name is a sobriquet attached to Polanski at the Rio de Janeiro Film Festival in 1969 "because of his size and irritating behavior."[62] The character makes his first appearance as Nancy is trying to excuse Alex's strange behavior to Jimmy. "Perhaps he had a difficult childhood," she offers, to which the as yet unseen Mosquito replies, "What about me?" and then adds, "That's no excuse for being a pain in the ass," reminding us of the frequent allusions to Polanski's own childhood in discussions about him and his work. After debunking such theories, Mosquito responds to Nancy's suggestion that Alex could be the victim of "obscure motives, some deep hidden trauma—" by exclaiming, "Trauma—balls!"

Mosquito's aggression is directed not only toward Nancy but also, through her, toward the audience—particularly the American audience.

Polanski has said that Nancy represents "something typically American,"[63] and he has repeatedly objected to Americans who attempt to overinterpret his symbolism and try to use his films to psychoanalyze him.[64] The name he has chosen for the character recalls Polanski's penchant for suggesting sexual frustration by means of buzzing flies. Mosquito goes about with a "big stinger." "You probably think it's something sexual," he accuses Nancy. But it is not; instead it is a large harpoon gun with which he steals articles of clothing and protects himself against others. "I don't like people getting in my way," he explains. This is Polanski at his most cynical, portraying the filmmaker as a lowly scavenger of other people's images. (Mosquito steals Nancy's T-shirt, as well as a stray tennis shoe.) His "equipment" is aggressively deployed as a substitute for the sexual obsessions that animate the others.

If Polanski the actor can deny the role of his sexuality, however, Polanski the director cannot. The art of earlier eras, such as *The Raft of the Medusa*, depicts extreme human suffering and need, deriving its passion from the conviction that there are values that make lives worth saving. By contrast, Polanski's modernist despair can only produce art that plays perverse games with his audience. After the director's arrest on charges of unlawful sexual intercourse with a minor, *What?* was recut and rereleased under the title *Diary of Forbidden Dreams* as a piece of soft-core pornography. The film's emphasis on sensational sexuality and its dismissal of emotional and intellectual levels of existence as valid expressions of meaning in contemporary life—or art—make it a prime candidate for such exploitation. In *What?* Polanski's commitment to a nihilistic modernism has led him to such extremes of ironic stylization that any substantive sociological or psychological issues are effectivelly bypassed. "I ask myself questions that get simpler and simpler every day," explains Joseph Noblart to Nancy at one point. "Alas, I realize that I'm less and less able to find the answers. In fact, it's getting so that I don't understand anything at all." The admission could be equally applied to the sensibility behind the film itself.

But such a hollow statement was not to be definitive in Polanski's oeuvre, for his cinematic personality was to be modified as his career progressed beyond modernism. His more commercial projects, in particular his popular horror films, helped to increase his rapport with the audience he often appears to despise. Through such encounters with the popular tradition he was forced to consider questions of sexuality and social process more deeply than he had ever done before.

3
The Human Subject:
Horror and the Popular Tradition

Horror and Its Audience

POLANSKI'S CAREER ENCOMPASSES both high art and popular entertainment. "I love the clichés," he has said. "Practically every film I
make starts with one. I just try to update them, give them an acceptable
shape."[1] While his absurdist projects represented, by and large, uncom-
promising modernist statements, his horror films have been created to
appeal to a mass audience. *Repulsion* was conceived as a potboiler that
could make financing available for *Cul-de-Sac; Rosemary's Baby* represented a chance to conquer Hollywood by filming a best-selling novel. In
a medium that involves vast sums of money, Polanski has taken care of
himself. But in so doing, he has also expanded the resources of his art.
The way he "updates" clichés—typically by tearing them out of their expected context and turning them against his audience—implicitly asks us
to confront the ways in which we use the institutions of popular genres
to express and disguise the structures of power underlying social
interaction.

"Among other things," critic Laura Mulvey has hypothesized, "the position of the spectators in cinema is blatantly one of repression of their
exhibitionism and projection of the repressed desire on to the performer."[2] In horror stories, this process typically operates through the creation
of a monstrous *other*, which, as Robin Wood has noted, represents "what
is repressed (but never destroyed) in the self and projected outward in
order to be hated and disowned."[3] Many such stories feature villains who
are racially or ethnically distinct from the "normal" heroes. With the exception of *Dance of the Vampires*, which parodies the genre in a lighthearted spirit, Polanski's tales of terror complicate this dynamic by
focusing on protagonists who are themselves "others," people trying to
make their way in alien worlds. In *Repulsion*, Carol Ledoux is a Belgian,
yet she lives in London; in *Rosemary's Baby*, a young, newly married
woman from the Midwest moves into a strange old New York City apartment building; in *The Tenant*, Trelkovsky, a Pole, tries desperately to survive in the hostile surroundings of Paris. Such a focus on social outsiders

*Polanski, playing an easily intimidated witness to horrific
happenings in* Dance of the Vampires, *attempts to vanquish a
vampire by driving a stake into his heart. Courtesy of the Film
Stills Archive, The Museum of Modern Art, New York.*

arouses complex reactions that mix sympathy with xenophobic contempt for people who do not conform to accepted social standards.

But if Polanski's horror films deal with outsiders *to* the worlds they portray, they are even more centrally concerned with the outsiders who invariably exist *within* these worlds: women. The presence of women in such stories raises cultural anxieties not only about social status but also about sexual identity.[4] Terrifying tales of female victimization have their roots in the Gothic fiction that flourished in later eighteenth-century Britain with works such as *The Castle of Otranto, The Monk,* and *The Mysteries of Udolpho.* Such tales continue today in the form of pulp novels and popular movies such as *Halloween.* Most often, these stories centered on "a shy, nervous, retiring heroine, who was nevertheless usually possessed of a remarkable ability to survive hideously dangerous situations."[5] No matter what happened, she never participated directly in the action. Pursued by unspeakable horrors, she was the object of desire and reward.[6] The hero was likely to be a powerfully masculine figure who, nevertheless, succumbed to the heroine's charms, thereby allowing the plot to be concluded harmoniously with a marriage. Such a narrative pattern displaces, and ultimately denies, female sexuality by surreptitiously encoding "perceptions about the subjugation of women and the covert social purposes of marriage and marital fidelity."[7]

In Polanski's horror films, women often become subjects rather than objects; consequently, their own sexuality is much more at issue. Both Carol Ledoux and Rosemary Woodhouse are plagued by demons inextricably connected with their femininity, Carol by her beauty and desirability to men, Rosemary by her pregnancy. And though *The Tenant* features a male rather than a female protagonist, his uncertain sense of gender identity becomes a major source of sexual conflict for him.

Unlike classic paradigms of the genre such as *Dracula* and *Frankenstein,* which usually take place in remote locales, Polanski's versions are typically set in modern urban environments. In contrast to the spare and bizarre locations of the modernist films, these settings include a wealth of plausible social and physical detail that encourages us to see the protagonists' problems within a believable context.

In Polanski's horror films, the role of society in creating situations that oppress the disenfranchised and lead women to repress and pervert their sexuality is openly addressed. *Repulsion* depicts a sexually grotesque culture in scenes set in the beauty parlor where the heroine works and in the pub where her boyfriend passes the time. *The Tenant* perceives society in terms of sadomasochistic interactions between bullying French landlords and victimized foreign tenants.

The protagonists of Polanski's horror films are oppressed not only by a bigoted society but also by a malevolent nature. Most strikingly, *Rosemary's Baby* uses its realistic mise-en-scène to suggest the ways in which an ordinary setting may gradually begin to appear menacing and portentous, even to an ostensibly normal heroine. Paradoxically, this increased emphasis on a realistic environment allows Polanski to explore individual psychology more intensely and completely than he could in the abstracted settings of the modernist films. For psychologies do not exist in isolation. As Lukács has suggested, people develop through contact with the world.

By focusing in these films on a single, fully developed individual within a recognizable setting, Polanski invokes many of the expectations of filmic realism. At the same time, however, the horror genre also poses an implicit challenge to realism, for it places the realist vision of plausible social interaction against a more primitive worldview that understands the universe in terms of magic and supernatural forces. Tzvetan Todorov's view of "the fantastic" as an ambiguous tension between the uncanny—in which the protagonist is insane—and the marvelous—in which the supernatural reigns supreme—is well expressed in Polanski's films.[8] *Repulsion* and *The Tenant* feature protagonists who are insane, while *Rosemary's Baby* offers a supernatural explanation for the bizarre situations it depicts. In each case, however, tension is built by playing on the ambiguous interactions between realism and fantasy.

The confusion between inner and outer reality engendered by "the fantastic" reflects modes of experience that are psychologically infantile, recalling a narcissistic period of development in which the individual was unable to distinguish itself from the world around it.[9] Polanski's horror films achieve their effect by reproducing such infantile states both in their protagonists and in their audiences. Thanks to his early interest in the surrealists, who experimented with the artistic depiction of unconscious thought processes, Polanski commands an impressive arsenal of resources with which he is able to express such confusion.[10]

Though all of Polanski's films are about insanity, in the horror films insanity is expressed in story lines that are more linear and complex than those of the modernist films. If the modernist films reproduce narcissistic anomie through stylized technique and caricatures of sexual obsession, the horror films, through their protagonists, trace the development of the regressive modes of relating inner and outer reality that lead to such states. Some of the modernist films hint at such narrative "development." The old woman in *When Angels Fall* harbors increasingly disturbed fantasies. The male protagonists of *Knife in the Water* and *Cul-de-Sac* turn from attempts at developing sexual relationships with their wives to more violent encounters with other men and finally to schizoid passivity as the action progresses. The horror films, however, develop this motif more fully. Carol Ledoux's tentative courtship in *Repulsion* gradually deteriorates into violence and catatonia. Alfred's romantic aspirations in *Dance of the Vampires* are eventually rewarded by having his beloved suck his body dry of blood. Rosemary Woodhouse's adoration of her handsome husband turns into a feeling of dread centered on the alien being that is growing inside her. Trelkovsky feels himself first an unwelcome tenant in his apartment building, his adopted country, and eventually within his own body. The heroes' frustrated attempts to achieve mature sexual fulfillment drive them back into a world of violence and rage that ultimately expresses itself in terms of fragmented body images and aberrant perceptions of the universe.

In the modernist works, the hero's ultimate powerlessness is normally expressed through static and objectified images. We watch from outside as George crouches fetally on a rock at the end of *Cul-de-Sac* and as Andrzej sits immobilized at the wheel of his car in *Knife in the Water*. In the horror films, however, Polanski exploits surrealistic techniques to express his heroes' conflicts subjectively, to encourage us to see the world in the distorted and fantastic vision of the protagonists. Though we may perceive the threatening quality of this world as the product of madness, it is nonetheless a madness we come to share intimately. Many shots show the protagonists in profile at the side of the frame, watching the action along with the spectators. Moreover, tracking shots accommodate to their movements more sympathetically than the coldly objective still camera camera setups Polanski favors in the modernist films.

In *Repulsion*, our terror at the sight of the catatonic Carol lying under the bed at the movie's conclusion is experienced in the context of our sympathetic understanding of her sexual disgust earlier in the film; we can participate in her anguish. Though Rosemary Woodhouse's paranoid sense of a conspiracy is ultimately validated, we are still moved by the way the specter of witchcraft forces her to look and behave more and more like an infant until at last she meekly submits her adult will to the authoritarian control of a group of Satanists. By contrast, we ultimately judge Trelkovsky insane in *The Tenant;* yet his early efforts at ingratiating himself with his callous neighbors and coworkers evoke our empathy. As T. J. Ross has noted, "the films place us in such relation to the inner circumstances of their wild protagonists as to open up for us perspectives on the everyday scene of an eerie acuity and intransigence."[11] As a result, we feel intimately involved in the fates of these characters. In contrast to the modernist films, which begin with images of the absurd and grotesque, anomalies emerge only gradually in the horror films. Initially everything appears natural; we—and the protagonists—are drawn into a more regressive mode.

Whether "sane" or "insane," all of the protagonists of the horror films are marked by a sense of disassociation between self and body. This sense is closely related to their feelings of sexual dis-ease. Polanski has developed ingenious methods of expressing this dis-ease while staying within the formula's realist conventions. In such regressed states, everything becomes an extension of the traumatic schism between body and self. Hence, images of fragmented or mutilated bodies abound. Many scenes in *Repulsion* open on extreme close-ups of body parts taken from unfamiliar angles. Frozen bodies reappear throughout *Dance of the Vampires*. Rosemary Woodhouse's body is misshapen by pregnancy. Trelkovsky disguises his body by creating a new one which is flamboyantly female.

This discomforting sense of physical alienation is also projected outward onto the environment. Accordingly, what often appears superficially as a natural mise-en-scène is revealed as a subjective expression of the protagonist's disturbed perception. The anthropomorphized apartments in which these characters live, with their dilating rooms and womblike corridors, update salient features of the large, looming castles in which horror stories have traditionally been enacted. In addition, images of rotting food and of repulsively wrinkled old people present the world as a terrifyingly real portrayal of psychotic perception.

When the environment is not perceived as an extension of a devalued body image, it is likely to be seen by these insecure characters as a threat to that image. The heroes of the horror films are obsessed with fantasies of "plots" against them, and Polanski's cinematography encourages similar fears in the spectator. The mise-en-scène often seems to be harboring hidden, portentous points of view. In one scene from *Dance of the Vampires* we watch a "horrifying" incident that features Alfred and Abronsius driving a stake into a vampire's heart. Their actions are, however, presented in silhouette as they move about behind a sheet. Though the camera soon reveals its joke (the two are actually rehearsing with a pillow), the message to the audience is clear: we may also be victimized by our partial vision of the action, which the director may "plot" in such a way as to punish us with shocking outbreaks of horror and violence.

The ambiguous nature of Polanski's realistic mise-en-scène surfaces dramatically at the moments when Polanski achieves the effect of deep space by means of extremely wide fish-eye lenses. Realistic depiction then gives way to a distorted vision that imposes menacingly on the spectator by reflecting the paranoid projections of disturbed sensibilities. In *Repulsion* Carol looks at her face reflected in a kettle and later watches the living room of her apartment yawn cavernously before her (an effect achieved, in this case, by the use of specially built sets as well as special lenses). The apartments of Rosemary Woodhouse and Trelkovsky take on similarly ominous dimensions as their inhabitants grow increasingly anxious, and the faces of others, too, degenerate into misshapen leers. Even Alfred in *Dance of the Vampires* is terrorized by the distorted features of Herbert, the lecherous homosexual vampire who has designs on the young man.

Such distorted images may also express the protagonists' distorted sexual desires. These characters often look out through peepholes or peek out of windows, attempting to see others without being seen by them. The director includes the audience in this descent into voyeuristic inactivity by presenting his characters themselves as objects of exhibitionistic display. These films all end with portraits within the cinematic text of audiences who coldly and sadistically view the protagonists as grotesque spectacles. In *Repulsion*, the Ledoux's neighbors gather around to gape at Carol's rigidly catatonic form. In *Dance of the Vampires*, the guests at the ball "catch out" the three main characters by isolating the images of their bodies in a mirror. In *Rosemary's Baby*, the members of the coven gathered in the Castevets' apartment quietly observe Rosemary as she wields a carving knife in a last, wildly extravagant attempt to save her baby. And *The Tenant* concludes by transforming the courtyard of Trelkovsky's building into a theater where the neighbors gather to applaud and jeer at the hero's suicide attempt.

These audiences mirror the response of the film's audience itself, which is increasingly encouraged to react to the protagonists in just this way, as alien and objectified "others," projections of forbidden impulses within ourselves. Polanski's vision is thus deepened by his confrontation with his traditional formula. His horror films do not simply illustrate cultural processes that victimize and warp the powerless; they ask us to recapitulate our own participation in such processes, and they expose the structures of domination that popular conventions naturalize. The subject of Polanski's horror films is not others, but otherness itself. This, apparently, is the kind of thing the director has in mind when he speaks of "updating" the clichés.

The Female Psyche: *Repulsion*

Polanski's explanation of the challenge *Repulsion* posed for him exemplifies his ambiguous approach to realism. "I have made a *tour de force*," he has insisted. "But this *tour de force* consisted essentially [in rendering] the story plausible, realistic. And I succeeded. . . . You will say what you please: everything is gross, silly, stupid, and anyone could tell the story in a grotesque manner. That is easy. Only I told it in a plausible manner, and with surprising psychological motivation. The result is that it has become true."[12] Some critics disagreed, echoing Harlan Ellison's opinion that the film's portrayal of aberrant psychology was "murky and unsatisfying. . . . To be entirely successful, a film of fear must deal with logic and the explanations that logic demands."[13] In fact, though the etiology of the heroine's illness is not explicitly spelled out, its development follows an exceptionally clear course. According to Gerard Brach, Carol's problem centers on her fear of sexuality, a favorite theme of Polanski's that takes a new direction in this film.[14]

The photograph of Carol's family, which we see twice, shows her alone and detached while her sister, Helen, rests her arms on the knee of a man, possibly their father. Part of Carol, we may assume, wishes to be her sister, which means embracing sexuality and the love of a man; another part, however, recoils from this desire, forcefully denying its existence, for to acknowledge it would mean inviting rejection both by the man, who in childhood preferred her sister, and by Helen herself.

As the action begins, increasing pressures have widened this split between desire and repression. Isolated in a foreign country, Carol is overwhelmed by a sense of alienation. And the admiration of men exacerbates her sexual anxiety. Her body, the tangible self with which she identifies her sense of rejection, becomes an object of hatred and shame to her. She tries to hide behind her hair, bites her nails. Fascinated, she gazes at the anamorphic reflection of her face in a kettle, a grotesque "false self" from which her inner being feels increasingly disassociated.

Helen has become Carol's only tie to her past and the only significant person in her life. With her shaky sense of her own identity, Carol is tempted to adopt that of her older sister, and the temptation is fostered by the behavior of others such as the landlord, who repeatedly confuses her with the "real" Miss Ledoux. When Helen leaves on a vacation, the pressure becomes intolerable; and Carol tries to replace her sister by becoming her sister, completing a cycle of narcissistic regression. She spends more and more time in her sister's bedroom, trying on Helen's cocktail dress, putting on her makeup, and ultimately relapsing into a state of catatonic self-negation under Helen's bed. To assume the mask of her sister is dangerous, for Helen's sexuality is both blatant and illegitimate: she is openly engaged in an affair with a married man. Nonetheless, Carol is enthralled by the possibility of mimicking Helen even while she is consumed with guilt. She projects the sexual desire that she takes on by means of hallucinations in which her body is forcibly molested by others. The first such hallucination appears as she is admiring herself in Helen's dress.

The object of Carol's sexual ambivalence is Michael, the most potent male presence in her environment and the man her sister possesses. The rabbit he has given Helen resembles a naked, inert fetus. Carol throws out Michael's toothbrush but compulsively sniffs at his razor and soiled undershirt. As if in response to her guilt over these carnal feelings, she receives an obscene phone call from Michael's wife (intended, significantly, for Helen), and sees a woman (again, probably Michael's wife) watching the apartment from the street. (Barbara Leaming reports that a scene in which Carol murders Michael's wife was edited out of the print before it was released, which explains the somewhat opaque references to her in the finished film.)[15] Obsessed with her increasingly violent internal conflicts, Carol is unable to see Colin, her would-be suitor, as anything more than a distraction and, eventually, as a threat. After killing him, she receives a picture postcard from Michael and Helen, who are vacationing in Pisa. The card features the leaning tower, which her sister has begged to see, along with a postscript from Michael, which reads, "Don't make too much *dolce vita* while we're away."

Unable to check the progress of her regression, Carol begins to hallucinate ever more wildly and is terrified. Prompted by the example of the virginal nuns who play innocent games outside her window, she adopts a childlike mode of behavior in an attempt to deny the intemperance of her desires. Abstractedly she sews and irons, improvising an increasingly mechanical performance of the role of a good little girl. Clad in her babyish nightdress, she ultimately resorts to lifeless passivity, at which point she is rewarded by finding herself at last in Michael's arms.

The film's final tracking shot looks again at objects in Carol's living room, the camera's smoothly integrating motion commenting ironically on the failure of these objects to form a coherent pattern. *Repulsion* ends by returning to the family portrait, the camera tracking in to an intense close-up of Carol's eye, reminding us of how close Polanski has brought us to her angle of vision. Yet, in a sense, the full secret of her consciousness can never be known; what we have seen in the film is merely, as the reporter puts it in *Citizen Kane*, "just a piece in a jigsaw puzzle." Though the piece we see forms a cogent pattern, such mental states possess an ultimately mysterious quality that Polanski does not try to deny. As Carol herself remains enigmatic, regardless of how much we understand about her, so are the objects that surround her ultimately mute, isolated, rationally inexplicable. No matter how violently we try to take hold of it, the world can only be experienced: it cannot be known.

Repulsion is thus a more radical work than might first be apparent. As Roy Armes has pointed out, "the film's combination of subjective viewpoint and objective observation in the context of a linear plot is less characteristic of modernist cinema than of the traditional approach to thriller structures of which Alfred Hitchcock is the master. But Polanski uses these devices not primarily to manipulate our responses to his story but as ends in themselves."[16] Yet *Repulsion* is not, as some early reviewers claimed, merely sensationalistic; it is about sensation, about the nature of our pleasure in the horror form.[17]

Repulsion defines not simply the psyche of a disturbed young girl but a sexually obsessed culture in which individuals confront each other as masters or slaves rather than as mutually affirming individuals. And it is a particular culture that is depicted rather than the kind of abstracted vision of "the human condition" that characterizes Polanski's modernist films. "One cannot film every subject everywhere," Polanski once commented. "Certain subjects are better suited to certain countries than to others. *Repulsion*, for example, is not a Polish subject. That is the way it is. It does not correspond to the climate of the country."[18] *Repulsion* is thus, in some sense, "about" Great Britain, about its society, and about a particular pop-

Carol crawls along the floor of her now cavernous apartment in Repulsion. *Courtesy of the Film Stills Archive, The Museum of Modern Art, New York.*

ular formula—the Gothic romance—which has flourished there for 150 years.

Much of the terror generated by *Repulsion* arises from the way Gothic conventions are evoked only to be unexpectedly overturned. Here the protagonist, not the setting, is exotic and unfamiliar. Her adventures are thereby placed in a context of psychological strain, strain that is aggravated by a cultural milieu in which behavioral expectations are clearly understood rather than mysterious. From Carol's perspective, we view an ordinary apartment as it becomes increasingly anthropomorphized to reflect the vague threats embodied in the looming, ominous castles found in more traditional generic models. Again the result is to reveal the genre's psychological underpinnings. For in *Repulsion*, Carol's passivity is no longer an attractively feminine response to a grotesque and threatening world but a pathological inability to integrate her own sexual desires into the realistic social milieu in which she finds herself.

Instead of fleeing, as the conventions approve, Carol attacks. Her sexual anxiety and confusion explode into a narcissistic rage that, in more conventional treatments, would have been projected onto villains with darkly obscure motives. Such reversals of conventional iconography are characteristic of the film. Though the traditional dark woman (Helen) may be, as often, sexually active, the fair young maiden (Carol), instead of being chaste, is sexually perverse. The chivalry of the wholesome young suitor (Colin) is exposed as a desire to control and manipulate rather than protect and nurture. Equally unsettling is the repulsive landlord, who continually badgers the beleaguered heroine to "pay the rent," but whose presumed position of power is rudely violated when the helpless maiden vigorously assumes the role of villain herself by murdering him. Polanski ends his film with a parody of the conventional image of a resolution in marriage: the white-gowned heroine is carried over the threshhold by the dark and brooding hero, but in this case the heroine is catatonic and the hero a cad. Thus *Repulsion* ironically comments on the vision of contained female sexuality that constitutes the denouement of previous Gothic tales.

By reversing the accepted conventions, the director reveals the perverse underpinnings of such popular narrative forms. In these stories, we are accustomed to a passive but seemingly normal heroine whose anxieties about her sexuality are projected onto the setting and action only to be relieved at the end through an image of socially sanctioned sexual possession in which she retains her "safe" position as the object rather than the perpetrator of desire. In *Repulsion*, however, we are confronted with a heroine whose passivity is patently unnatural and with the sexual polarization of a male-dominated culture that casts her and other women, such as Helen and Bridget, into the roles of sexual objects and sexual victims.

Insofar as society itself appears oppressive, Carol's withdrawal from it seems the most normal conceivable response.[19] The picture Polanski gives us of Carol's milieu seems initially a plausible and acceptable one: it strikes us as a reasonable presentation of the way Western society operates. Yet sexuality dominates virtually every aspect of life. All the casual socializing we see occurs in sex-segregated settings: a beauty shop and a pub. The beauty shop where Carol is employed is devoted to the rites of sexual exhibitionism, and its often grotesque inhabitants are obsessed alternately with their desirability to men and with their vulnerability to them. Even on the street, a woman's body is on display, to be assessed and commented on by any man who chooses to do so—as Carol's is early in the film. Women appear here as trapped by the fact that sexual acceptance by a male is the most available option that society can offer them for fulfillment.

The nature of this acceptance is of dubious value. "Men want to be spanked, and then given sweets," asserts one of the clients at the beauty parlor, offering a view of sexuality that emphasizes sadomasochism. In a like-minded spirit, Bridget glows when she reports that her boyfriend "was practically on his knees" to her. And in a less narrowly sexual vein, she recounts with obvious relish and amusement a scene from *The Gold Rush* that centers on cannibalism. Similarly, Helen tells a "funny story" about the Minister of Health, who "found eels coming out of his sink." She entertains herself by watching boxing on television—like Chaplin films, a "harmless" amusement that assumes a darker significance in the context of Polanski's emphasis on perverse sexuality here.

Such attitudes characterize the male sphere as well. In the pub, Colin's friend Reggie reacts enthusiastically to a tale told by his companion John about two women fighting "like those women wrestlers in Hamburg." Encouraged by Reggie's interest, John offers to introduce him to his cousin, a "black belt" karate expert. This suggestion so excites Reggie that he continues to badger John about it for the remainder of the scene, watched all the while by a bartender standing silently in the background. Significantly, Carol is not present during this exchange; nor is she affected by it later: we witness it merely as a brief sketch of the prevailing sexual mores among "normal" young men.

In *Repulsion* society at large is caught up in a pattern of male exploitation and female victimization, from the men at the pub and the women at the beauty shop to the more intimate portrait of Michael and Helen's relationship, in which Michael uses his economic power to buy his mistress's acquiescence. Evenings out and vacations are casually purchased while a wounded and betrayed wife skulks in the background. At the film's end, the sighs of pleasure we have earlier heard from Helen while she was making love are eerily echoed in her gasps of terror and pain. Michael responds to these latter sounds by slapping her, grotesquely parodying the underlying power dynamic of their sexual relationship.

Even the mild-mannered, well-intentioned Colin finds himself drawn into the dominance-submission pattern that characterizes the film's romantic attachments. Though, as far as we can see, he has received no encouragement at all from Carol, his friends, speaking as arbiters of socially accepted mores, conclude that she is simply "teasing," and that she "gets a big thrill out of it." As a remedy, they advise an evening drinking gin in Reggie's apartment with "three of the most eligible bachelors in London" to provide her with even bigger thrills. Though disgusted by their suggestion, Colin feels justified in assuming that as a chivalrous man in love it is appropriate for him to try every means in his power to break down the defenses of the object of his desire.

Later, the thick-skinned landlord is even more dramatically misled by his culturally derived attitudes about female passivity. Though Carol greets him in a state of semicatatonia, barely able to function, he reads her behavior as a sexual provocation; her carelessness about her person, an invitation; her lack of energy, acquiescence. Because she seems sexually unprotected, she appears sexually available—and therefore sexually conquerable. Her very disintegration constitutes her attractiveness. By comparison, Colin's excitement in the face of her unresponsiveness is different in degree but not in kind. In the face of such exploitation, the power of female lust is most properly expressed in terms of madness and mayhem—and finally as catatonic self-abnegation. Thus seen, the murders in Polanski's film are acts of unconscious sexual terrorism, while the final image of marriage is seen as an act of sexual secession. It is an extreme view of the opposing forces of rampant female desire and suffocating cultural expectations.

Repulsion's investigation of social practice and psychological breakdown also implicates its audience, for Polanski's realistic technique forces us to share Carol's experience. "One enters a landscape," he has said of the film, "a landscape of the mind."[20] The terror we feel in *Repulsion* is ultimately generated by the extent to which we identify with the viewpoint of the film's protagonist—and thereby are brought close to our own impulses toward schizoid withdrawal and even murder.[21]

At a more universal level, our ability to share the perceptions of a heroine whom we understand to be insane calls the very conception and value of normalcy itself into question, for in *Repulsion* Polanski puts his heroine—and his audience—"at an angle to the everyday scene which is close to that of a poet."[22] Is Carol simply disturbed, or does she see the world around her with an oblique clarity? *Repulsion* exploits the eccentricity of its heroine's perceptions to show us an unfamiliar face of a familiar world, and thereby attacks the belief in a benign and rational universe. The surrealist-inspired images of raw meat, razors, and an eyeball slit by the opening credits gradually escalate to more violent episodes that disrupt the orderly flow of the narrative. Such images defamiliarize the quotidian and imply a pain and violence beneath the civilized surface.

The opening shot of the heroine's eye explicitly invites the spectator to identify with her point of view, and the montage immediately following features fragmented images of body parts: a gnarled hand adorned with an ornate ring, a face seen upside down covered with a grotesque "beauty" mask (the latter a mummified representation of death portending the more pervasive preoccupation with Egyptology in *The Tenant*). Such images are repulsive and disorienting, but they are in no way implausible. Later they are followed by others, which are equally bizarre: a rotting potato sprouting roots, a skinned rabbit ready to be cooked, a strange trio of musicians, one of whom walks backward. Also in keeping with schizophrenic perception is the hyperesthesia communicated by the exaggerated presence of everyday sounds: buzzing flies, the dripping of a faucet, a ticking clock. And Chico Hamilton's frenetic, slightly dissonant jazz score reinforces the film's ambience of dislocation and angst. Here again, the sinister overtones of the abnormal in the normal are played upon to make Carol's reactions feel horrifyingly appropriate.

Polanski, initially at least, conveys a state of abnormality simply by emphasizing the monstrous aspects of everyday life, not only through his choice of images and sounds but also through framing and editing. The fragmentation of the initial montage is repeated in sudden cuts to huge close-ups of body parts before the entire body is comfortably situated within a larger environment by means of an establishing shot: Helen's black-gloved hand resting on Carol's shoulder; the plump face of a middle-aged woman being sprayed with liquid; the hideously contorted mouth of Colin's friend John. Later the effect is terrifyingly reproduced following the murder of Colin, whose twitching hand and bleeding skull seen in isolation deny his body the integrity and wholeness that would allow us to empathize with his humanity. What is reproduced is a vision of things and parts of things in isolation from one another and a fragmenting of body image, which lies at the heart of the schizoid view of reality.

The infantile inability to separate the self from its environment also finds expression in the anthropomorphic presentation of the Ledoux apartment. Its increasingly cavernous living room and long, constricting hallways reveal Carol's vacuous sense of herself. The kitchen and bath service physical needs, and the images associated with them—unwholesome food, unhygienic accoutrements—graphically communicate the disgust and rejection of bodily functions Carol is experiencing. The pattern created by the wallpaper and bedspread in her own bedroom is prisonlike, expressive of her ascetic self-denial, whereas the quarters of her sexually self-indulgent sister are marked by frills, mirrors, and a prominently placed bed.

During the latter part of the film, this resonant ambiguity is occasionally sacrificed for the sake of depicting the more extreme expressions of madness. At this point the sight of cracking plaster and hands coming out of the walls appears to many viewers "gratuitous, old-fashioned and derivative."[23] At such moments *Repulsion's* delicately balanced relationship between internal and external reality begins to break down, and we may see the heroine as a case study rather than a surrogate eye. But Polanski's carefully controlled ambiguity between the objective and subjective viewpoint prevails, reaching a climax when Colin mounts an assault on the Ledoux apartment. Our feelings by this time are confused and conflicted. We are afraid for him; but we are also afraid of him. Though we are by this time aware enough of Carol's psychological disintegration to fear her response to this invasion, our sympathy with her point of view enables us to share her experience of the break-in as a rape. The confusion between internal and external phenomena that encourages this perception is em-

phasized by the frighteningly distorted view of Colin we share with the
heroine as she peers through the eyelike aperture of the apartment door.
Shrinking into a fetal position at the far corner of the entryway, Carol
watches with us as the entrance into her sanctuary is brutally violated.
Her subsequent defense of herself comes as a relief as well as an outrage.
Such a conclusion calls into question the audience's motives for partici-
pating in such fantasies—and especially our relationship to this particular
variation. From the beginning our customary attitude of sanguine passivity has been violently attacked. The film's opening image showing us an
eye bisected by the credits, recalls the slashed eyeball in *Un Chien An-
dalou* (1925), an early savage exposé of the unconscious underpinnings of
our pleasure in watching movies. Just as the film's generic reversals impli-
cate us by upsetting our customary emotional patterns, so its visual strategies probe our role as passive observers.

In *Repulsion*, the audience cannot help but feel threatened by the danger to the seeing eye. For Carol also watches; and she, like us, wishes to
do so with impunity: that is one way in which her passivity is defined.
Before we share her view of Colin through the peephole of her apartment
door, we share another stolen glance at the old lady who lives across the
hall. Carol also looks out of her window at the nuns playing in the courtyard below her apartment and at Michael's wife down on the street. At the
same time, like the audience, she tries to avoid the looks of others; she
hides behind her hair, a strategy the camera complies with by repeatedly
shooting her so that her face is obscured. But her attempts prove fruitless,
for she is unable, ultimately, to protect herself from becoming an object in
the eyes of men—and of the audience.

The fatal candlestick by which Carol punishes Colin assails the camera
directly, for as Carol has been violated by the gazes of others within the
film, so has she been by ours. For we have not merely been watching with
Carol; we have also been watching Carol. Played by beautiful Catherine
Deneuve, she is often perceived by Polanski's camera as an aesthetically
pleasing presence rather than a full human being. Carol's immobile features encourage such a response. The spectator's participation in the film
thereby involves not only empathy with Carol's sexual desires but also enjoyment of her sexual objectification.

At the end of *Repulsion*, as happens in so many Polanski films, we find
an audience much like ourselves, pleased to gape at a gruesome spectacle
of distress and ruin—for our impulse to look is revealed ultimately as hostile. One old man goes to peer at the corpse of the landlord in the living
room. And Michael stares in fascination at Colin's putrefying remains in
the bathtub. At last, as he carries her across the threshhold, Michael also
shares a look with Carol, a look of peculiar understanding and complicity.
In effecting a complete transformation into an object by her lapse into
catatonia, she finally establishes a clandestine rapport with him.

Carol's breakdown, in fact, has been triggered by a sense of her own position in the world as a physical object to provide surreptitious sexual gratification to others while her own desires are denied. Though at least one critic has objected to the director's "sadistic attitude toward his heroine,"[24] it is an attitude appropriate to the purposes of the film. For it is also, in part, the audience's attitude. In *Repulsion* our desire to look without ourselves being the subject of a reciprocating gaze is horrifyingly exposed as a desire to objectify, control, even to destroy. In the world of *Repulsion*, which is a world we recognize as a valid re-creation of contemporary Western culture, there may be pity, but there is also terror.

The Celebration of Childhood: *Dance of the Vampires*

As a personal project based on principles of parody and eccentricity, *Dance of the Vampires* could be considered with Polanski's modernist projects. Yet, the genre it parodies is the horror story. Though it is certainly quite different from his more realistic versions of the formula, it nevertheless sheds significant light on this aspect of Polanski's development. Besides raising many of the sexual and social issues Polanski's other horror films address, it also develops a relatively cogent narrative and creates, in the character of Alfred, a central figure more empathic than any of the protagonists in the modernist films.

The production history was marked by more than the usual number of setbacks and last-minute changes. Though it was originally scheduled to be shot at a chateau in the Dolomites, the lack of snow in the Italian alps led to the project's being moved back to the studio in England. MGM, the film's distributor, specified that it be produced in a 1:85 ratio, but after most of the footage had been shot, Polanski decided to blow it up to Panavision dimensions, thereby giving some of the exteriors a grainy appearance.

The most serious problem the production encountered arose after shooting had been completed; the producer Martin Ransohoff edited Polanski's print for American distribution and retitled it *The Fearless Vampire Killers*. When the film was finally released in the United States in 1967, a crude cartoon had been added to the opening, the voices of the characters played by Jack MacGowran and by Polanski himself had been redubbed, the music had been changed, and twenty minutes' worth of material, much of it showing voyeuristic activity crucial to the movie's thematic thrust, had been excised. The director has made several bitter comments about Ransohoff's unauthorized tampering, and has justified his case by pointing to the greater commercial success enjoyed abroad by his own version of the film.[25]

The movie's spritely ambience is suggested by its title. Along with *What?*, it is the lightest of Polanski's creations, cloaking his characteristic preoccupations with troubled sexuality and debilitating power relationships in a childlike costume of parody and make-believe. "It's a fairy tale to me," he has said. "It's close to a cartoon or a trip to Disneyland."[26] Its once-upon-a-time opening narration is heard over a picturesque, snow-covered landscape that gradually fades from a painted backdrop to an almost equally unrealistic-looking set. Krzysztof Komeda's choral music accompanied by sleighbells completes the Disney-ish spirit. Polanski leans more toward pastels here than in any of his other films. Fast-motion photography gives the chase sequences a feeling of animation, and the excitement of the chases is enhanced by Wilfred Shingleton's ingenious sets for the castle, with their mazes of corridors and low parapets carefully graduated to maximize the visibility of the pursuers and the pursued. The playful cartoon spirit is further suggested by the prevalence of long and medium shots, which replace the intense, claustrophobic close-ups the director customarily favors.

As a parody of its genre, *Dance of the Vampires* offers a provocative critique of vampires and the stories about them. Traditionally such creatures have appeared as avatars of an undefined malignity, terrorizing humanity with strange threats of death and transmogrification. Polanski's vampire tale, which follows the adventures of Professor Abronsius and his assistant Alfred as they penetrate the castle of the sinister Count Von Krolock in the forests of Transylvania, follows the classic pattern closely. The director has commented on his use of recent versions of the formula produced by Hammer studios in Britain as models, especially *Brides of Dracula* (1960). His own film cleverly mimics many of the visual and narrative motifs of these models, which themselves satirize the genre. "I stylized a style," Polanski claimed.[27]

Vampire legends recall a period of rigid class hierarchies, and *Dance of the Vampires* generates considerable humor by wryly parodying the genre's sentimentalized portraits of class differences. In traditional vampire stories, peasants—except for their picturesque costumes—retain few of the realistic trappings of their station. The peasants gathered in the inn at the beginning of Polanski's film, however, are a pathetic group: old, ragged, and dun-colored. There is even a slack-mouthed idiot plucking a chicken.

The vampires' hold over them is based on inherited privilege, which carries with it a droit du seigneur. The portraits in Von Krolock's castle, which we see at some length during Alfred and Abronsius's first visit there—and indeed, the age of the castle itself—attest to the venerability of his tenure. The aristocratic Von Krolock's sway over the community ultimately rests on magic, and *Dance of the Vampires* creates a world in which supernatural qualities are tangible forces—in nature as well as in society. The vampire represents a demonic feudalism that preys on ordinary Transylvanians and dominates in a religious way even the community of vampires. Von Krolock is a grim pastor who addresses his congregation of fellow vampires with the words, "Dearly beloved brethren." His victims are initiated into the secret order of which he is high priest.

To oppose Von Krolock, Polanski develops the character of Professor Abronsius, whose association with scientific rationality is pitted against the vampire's connection with the supernatural. As a variation of the scientist figure traditional to the vampire formula, the professor is modeled on such figures as Dr. Von Helsing in Bram Stoker's *Dracula*. As Ivan Butler has pointed out, not only Von Krolock but also Abronsius abuses a position of power.[28] Alfred, the professor's assistant, bears the brunt of this abuse. These two figures recall the two characters in Polanski's early short feature *The Fat and the Lean* (in which the director also played the role of the servant). Though Abronsius maintains a benign and comic presence, he thoughtlessly exploits Alfred. As his assistant precariously carries him across the castle ramparts, he speaks rapturously of the sunset; and he remains blithely unconcerned about Alfred's terror of the vampires as well as about his assistant's longing to rescue the innkeeper's pretty daughter Sarah from their clutches. Ultimately, however, the professor does save Sarah for Alfred's sake, and the benign promise generated by his comic presence triumphs. The satiric bite of his exploitative attitude toward his servant is also softened by the similar attitude he holds toward himself. Upon meeting the fearsome Von Krolock, he is chiefly absorbed by the vampire's acuity on the esoteric topic of bats, which Abronsius has devoted his life to studying. His "dispassionate" intellectuality means that he is oblivious even to his own welfare.

In their way, Von Krolock and Abronsius play the roles of bad and good father figures traditional in vampire stories.[29] And, in a sense, the entire film is based on a double entendre that pokes fun at the horror genre: while the professor, the good father figure, is taken up with the surface of the narrative—overcoming the mysterious power of the vampires—the deeper meaning is represented by Von Krolock, the bad father figure who acts out the regressive sexual fears and wishes that generate such stories.

At times this double structure emerges explicitly in the film's humor. Abronsius is comic in part because he is obtuse: at one level, he fails to understand what the film is about. Whenever a situation displays erotic overtones, he is invariably looking elsewhere. After the two travelers first arrive at the inn, Alfred gapes down at the half-exposed breasts of Magda, the serving girl, as she bathes his feet while the oblivious professor gazes intently up at the garlic that has been placed on the ceiling to repulse the vampires. Later, when looking through the telescope, the single-minded professor turns away upon discovering Shagal, the innkeeper, climbing up to Magda's room. Earlier, when Shagal goes up to the attic at night to visit Magda, Abronsius excitedly pursues him, expecting to discover more clues about vampirism—only to find himself hit over the head with an enormous, phallic sausage by Shagal's jealous wife, Rebecca. Later, the stake that is to be used to destroy the vampires also becomes a sexually charged object during the exchange between Abronsius and Rebecca. ("Stick it in?" Rebecca asks, examining the stake suspiciously. "Stick it in where?")

The professor's obtuseness about sexual issues is closely related to his disassociation from his own body. His pratfalls, ungainly posturings, and general clumsiness are engaging evidences of his unconcern and consequent lack of control over the physical functions he must perform as a human being. At the same time, however, he often displays an unexpected physical agility. Upon embarking to the vampire's castle, he skis down a long hill into Alfred's waiting arms. Later, to find the vampires' coffins, he gingerly tiptoes across the castle ramparts. Before bed, he sinuously scratches his back on the bedpost, and on rising, he jumps into his pants. (This last stunt required over forty takes before actor Jack MacGowran could perform it to Polanski's satisfaction.) These remarkable feats seem to be executed by a body that is beyond his control. "They flap their vital limbs without thinking," Abronsius explains to Von Krolock, describing the way bats can fly while asleep. At the same time, he begins, absently, to flap his own elbows, as if to take flight himself. The association between this sort of physical dexterity and sexual energy is explicitly made by Von Krolock as he watches Shagal bring Magda into the castle. "An old man with his flabby stomach and spindly legs bringing with doglike devotion a young damsel who only a few nights ago was under his protection," observes the Count. "See how he struts and capers."

It is Alfred, however, played by Polanski himself, upon whom the theme of sexual dis-ease centers. Like the protagonists of Polanski's other horror films, he regresses from mature romantic ambitions to infantile passivity and defeatedness. Alfred initially appears as a moonstruck youth, who idealizes the innocence and purity of Sarah, the innkeeper's daughter. But passivity and impotence fight with his desire and ultimately overcome it. He is scarcely able to speak to Sarah. Faced with the awesome stake, which he is expected to drive into the vampires' hearts, he blanches with terror and later loses it altogether.

Alfred repeatedly substitutes seeing for more direct sexual involvement. He first glimpses Sarah accidentally as she is bathing. (Her predilection for taking baths distinguishes her from the realm of the grubby, physically repugnant peasants he has encountered earlier.) Later he sees her through the keyhole as her father spanks her for unwittingly exhibiting herself in front of his guests. At night, he spies on Count Von Krolock attacking Sarah, an eroticized encounter that leaves a bloodstain on the bath bubbles. In a state of childish terror over the traumatic enactment of defloration he believes he has witnessed, the young man appeals to the professor for help.

In the vampire's castle, Alfred tries again to establish contact with Sarah but finds, to his horror, that he, as heterosexual voyeur, has become the feminized object of another man's voyeurism—and lust. Herbert, the Count's homosexual son, repeatedly leers openly at the young apprentice with undisguised sexual interest. Herbert's baby blue garments complement Alfred's effeminate pink socks, red bow tie, and wine-colored coat. When they are alone together, Alfred is terrified to find his reflection in the mirror unaccompanied by that of his companion: he is alone, exposed, a helpless object of unwanted desire, open to be viewed but unable to reciprocate the look. Alfred's frantic attempt to escape by running around the balcony only brings him back to the same threat he has been trying to get away from: he cannot escape from Herbert's—and the camera's—gaze. After the two tussle briefly on the floor of the hallway (in an encounter eroticized by Herbert's suggestive nightshirt), Alfred again escapes to the security of the professor.

Yet even this relationship, for all of its facade of innocence and disinterested scholarly enterprise, is problematic. The two men are first seen together wrapped in scarves like two old women. After we see Shagal in bed with his wife, Polanski cuts in a shot of Alfred and Abronsius's bedtime activities: in a parody of sadomasochistic sexual foreplay, Alfred is curing boils by putting heated glass cups on the professor's back as the elderly scholar lies reading. Later, in the Count's castle, Alfred even attempts to get into bed with his master, much to Abronsius's outrage. Though their affection for one another is not explicitly sexual, it represents Alfred's childlike retreat into intimacy with a figure of his own sex who is at the same time like a parent.

In spite of the professor's safe parental chastity, however, this relationship, too, fails Alfred as his passivity grows in response to the terrors that surround him. His sense of physical integrity gradually erodes. Invited by Abronsius to look through a telescope in the castle, he focuses on Saturn, a symbol of sluggishness and impotence—in marked contrast to the inviting close-up of the moon, a symbol of vampirish eroticism and romance, which opened the film. He loses one of his mittens when it is pierced by an iron spike on the castle gate. Later, he loses the stake with which he is to destroy his enemies. And, at the end of the film, his shoe comes off as Sarah's embrace draws the very blood from his body.

Alfred's retreat from mature sexuality is made sympathetic by the style of the film as a whole. Discomfort with the body is suggested by the images of stiffly frozen, lifeless figures that reappear throughout the action. Images of physical repulsiveness abound, culminating in the vision of the count's servant Koukol, clubfooted and hunchbacked, who replaces Alfred in Sarah's vision as she gazes out her window. Characteristically, Polanski associates this imagery with the carnality of the vampires: they become repulsive when they bare their fangs, and they appear even more disgusting after having gorged themselves on blood. As the schism between cerebral purity and gross bestiality widens, the film's colors polarize, evolving from seductive pastel and natural flesh tones in the early scenes to the drab colors and sickly skin tones that dominate in Von Krolock's castle. Sarah herself changes dramatically, from a rosy-cheeked maiden dressed in white to a pale-skinned woman with startlingly red hair and a vivid scarlet dress—a personification of the popular image of an oversexed person.

Alfred's voyeuristic impulse to displace sexual energy into the act of watching rather than to participate directly in sexual activity is repeatedly emphasized by shots of other characters peering through windows, keyholes, and telescopes. And anxiety about watching may also lead to anxiety about being watched. When Alfred first enters Von Krolock's castle with Professor Abronsius, he confides guiltily, "I have a funny feeling we are being watched." And indeed, they are. Polanski's deep-focus photography shows us Koukol staring at the two intruders, though their own angle of vision momentarily prevents them from understanding that they have been trapped. Later, a similar effect is achieved through sound. As Alfred and Abronsius gaze over a parapet to see the vampires rising out of their graves, a voice behind them announces, "You should never have come here." "Then why *did* we come?" inquiries Alfred, assuming the voice to have been that of the professor. But the two then turn to discover what the audience already knows: that the voice belongs to Von Krolock, who has trapped them again.

The hidden meanings that threaten Alfred may also threaten the audience. When the apprentice and the professor first enter Shagal's inn, an imbecilic peasant naively begins to tell them about Von Krolock's castle, only to be silenced summarily by his neighbor. Meanwhile, another man, black-eyed and sinister, steps between the imbecile and the camera to gaze threateningly at the "outsiders"—and at us. Polanski thus suggests his own ability to manipulate what is seen and understood for his own ends, which may not necessarily be benign.

Finally the image is most frightening for its very failure to render a perceived evil, as the two scenes in which vampires are not reflected in mirrors imply. Alfred's terror over Herbert's attempted "seduction" crystallizes around his startling discovery that his image has been captured in a mirror without that of the vampire: he can be observed while Herbert cannot. Later, at Von Krolock's ball, Alfred and the professor can mingle undetected among the vampires, but in the grand procession toward the mirrored wall the vampires, while still all around them, abruptly lose their image. The mirrors reflect Alfred, Abronsius, and Sarah in isolation from the lecherous vampires—exposed and vulnerable to the audience *in* the film as well as the audience *of* the film by virtue of their very physicality.

Dance of the Vampires ends with a shot of the professor looking ahead as he drives the sleigh out of Transylvania while Polanski's camera shows the audience that, in the back of the sleigh, Sarah is infecting Alfred with vampirism. "Professor Abronsius never guessed he was carrying away with him the very evil he had wished to destroy," the narrator tells us. "Thanks to him this evil would at last be able to spread across the world."

This last image contains even more chilling implications when considered politically, for Abronsius and Alfred are German, and Sarah is Jewish.[30] Her father's name, Shagal, is a variation on that of painter Marc Chagall. Chagall's art often mythologizes the shtetl life of his youth in turn-of-the-century Vitebsk, a town in the Russo-Polish Pale, which, after enduring a century of pogroms, was destroyed by the Nazis. Polanski's portrayal of Shagal's terror thus makes fantasy out of a threat that is closely connected with traumatic memories of the director's own childhood, memories he shares with Chagall. Such a treatment of the vampire legend adds an explicitly racial dimension to its themes of class and sexuality.

Yet such disturbing implications never overwhelm the prevailing spirit of fairy-tale innocence. The final dance sequence, from which the film derives its title, is depicted in a series of extended tracking shots, revealing a complicated and harmonious synchronization between graceful bodies in motion and an accommodating camera. Like Chagall, Polanski uses his art here to mythologize and idealize his early experiences. The pervasive window imagery the two artists share suggests their common commitment to a fanciful vision of a reality constructed by their prismatic imaginations. Though Polanski's imagination often creates darker fantasies than those depicted in Chagall's paintings, in *Dance of the Vampires* this darkness is subsumed by a Chagallian delight in the glowing colors of a more joyful childhood.

The Trauma of Infancy: *Rosemary's Baby*

Rosemary's Baby represented, for Polanski, a chance to prove himself in Hollywood, "the place that belonged more to my dreams than to my reality, at the threshold of where everything would be handed to me."[31] His name was put forward for the project by Robert Evans, then an executive at Paramount, who had been impressed by *Repulsion*. Hollywood producer William Castle, who owned the rights to Ira Levin's best-selling novel and had originally wanted to use it for his own directing debut, agreed to let Polanski do the project after the young Polish filmmaker enthusiastically pledged to adapt the book with a minimum number of changes. Polanski wrote the screenplay himself with some assistance from the film's designer, Richard Sylbert. The project was a great success, both critically and commercially, making over $30 million and spawning a whole genre of enormously popular devil-child pictures such as *The Ex-*

Over Vitebsk *by Marc Chagall (1915–20). Courtesy of the Collection, The Museum of Modern Art, New York.*

orcist and *The Omen.*[32] As a consequence, Polanski became a highly bankable commodity in the world's film capital. And though the director was later to comment that the film was "less personal because it didn't start as my project,"[33] he found ways of incorporating his own concerns into the finished product.

Levin's 1967 book describes a young, newly married woman who is impregnated by the devil shortly after moving into the Bramford, a strange old apartment building inhabited by witches. The story encouraged Polanski to examine further the psychology of a complex individual who exists within a coherent social and physical environment. Like *Dance of the Vampires, Rosemary's Baby* takes us back to childhood. But instead of delighting us with juvenile fantasy, this film horrifies us by realistically reinvoking a sense of the powerlessness engendered by an infantile confusion between fantasy and reality.

The fears aroused by *Rosemary's Baby* ultimately take the form of infantile terrors centering on bodily integrity. The film turns the conventional cinematic clichés of "innocent" childish experience back on themselves to reveal a world in which the psychological and the factual are terrifyingly indistinguishable. The novel, by contrast, displaces this psychological issue onto the physical universe. In the book Rosemary's problem is not that she has the "pre-partum crazies," as her actor-husband, Guy, suggests, but that there is an actual plot against her instigated by the devil himself. By being encouraged to attribute these phenomena to the workings of supernatural powers, we are reassured about the disturbing connotations of Rosemary's emotional state.

Though Polanski's screenplay stays close to Levin's original story, the movie maximizes the ambiguity between paranoid projection and real events that the novel repeatedly strives to resolve. Among Polanski's films it is most similar to *Repulsion*, from which it borrows much of its iconography, most importantly its anthropomorphized depiction of the Woodhouses' apartment. Here, however, in place of the insane heroine of *Repulsion*, a diabolical universe is ultimately exposed. But in both cases, the audience's growing uncertainty about the nature of the reality being presented creates suspense and involvement. Though Polanski initially takes pains to establish a strong sense of verisimilitude, as the narrative proceeds, this initially credible facade increasingly polarizes into two divergent choices: perverse projection or diabolical plot.

The audience leaves the theater with a strong sense that the narrative has validated the heroine's vision of a "plot," an effect that has led many critics to comment that the film actually diminishes the ambiguity of the novel.[34] And at a certain level, this is true. The world Polanski has created is filled with paranoid images. He often shoots his characters flanked by the strong verticals of the apartment's doorways, which visually constrict them. Near the end, we feel Rosemary's entrapment even more powerfully because of the film's imagery of imprisonment. When the evidence seems overwhelmingly to point to the Castevets' guilt, Rosemary appears in a gray and white striped dress and is put to nap by Dr. Hill on a similarly striped couch while the barlike shadows of the venetian blinds fall across her face. Though such images present the heroine as clearly and unambiguously trapped, we may overlook the question of *what* is trapping her.

Examined more closely, however, the film offers a good deal of evidence that the trap exists within herself. Polanski makes her psychological vulnerability more plausible by isolating her from her family and from any benign neighbors, both of whom provide her with a certain security in the novel. But the triggering mechanism of her breakdown is her pregnancy. Later, when her baby is born, the source of her anxiety shifts from terror that part of her objectified body could be appropriated by others to an ambivalent hatred/attraction toward the part of her body that is no longer hers, a response Ellen Moers has called "the motif of revulsion against newborn life."[35] Accordingly, she sees her baby first as endangered, then as diabolical.

To Rosemary, pregnancy represents the public avowal of her sexuality.[36] The viewer is alerted to the issue of sexual repression early in the film when Guy playfully caresses his wife's back in the elevator on their way up to view the apartment. Polanski follows the gesture with a close-up of the elevator attendant looking at them ominously. Shortly afterward, when her husband kisses her in the kitchen of their prospective home, Mr. Niklas, the building superintendent, comments from the next room, "No, no, no, no, not in the apartment!" Though he is referring to an earlier question about where the previous tenant had died, his exclamation suggests the embarrassment connected with open displays of sexual passion. Later, the heroine's dreams of her Catholic girlhood include the figure of a disapproving nun. When she is first told of her pregnancy, she herself wears a nunlike white-collared black dress, as she had done on her first visit to her sinister neighbors the Castevets, when she defended the Pope.

Yet, though Rosemary is anxious about sexuality, she also desires it. To resolve her dilemma, she conjures up an image of power and violence that is both erotic and punitive: a diabolical rapist. Ernest Jones has formulated the problem: "Sometimes voluptuous feelings are coupled with those of *angst*; especially with women, who often believe that the night fiend has copulated with them."[37] While being raped by what she imagines as the devil, Rosemary is aware that her reaction is observed by the nude coven, pictured through wide-angle distortion, which suggests grotesque fantasy. Following this dream of sadistic and guilty sexuality we see her in bed while her husband is sleeping, as if to emphasize her emotional and physical isolation from him.

After confirming that she is indeed pregnant, Rosemary finds her body strange and repulsive. She begins to feed it disgusting foods: raw meat and an unpalatable-looking drink made for her by Minnie Castevet. Soon she tries to deny her sexuality by assuming the pose of a presexual child: to avoid facing the fact that she is having a baby, she becomes a baby. The winsome, ingenuous presence of Mia Farrow is used to good effect to help make this transition credible. As her body grows more distended, she has her hair cut to a babyish length by Vidal Sassoon.

As the heroine's figure changes, idealized representations of bodies begin to intrude into the pictorial compositions, suggesting Rosemary's increasing estrangement from her own body. A slim, long-legged nude statue occupies an important position in the frame when Rosemary is feeling unwell on the first day of her period, and we see the statue again as she sits in front of the TV set doubled over in pain, watching women dancers moving in perfect synchronization. Polanski associates a second, limbless statue with Guy, who rehearses for a new role on crutches, a visual symbol of impotence. "I'm in love with no-one, especially not your fat wife," he says. "I'm a hopeless cripple." Rosemary, who arrives home from Vidal Sassoon's in time to hear this speech, later adopts more childish clothing and loses weight. Her more immediate response, however, is to announce that she is in pain. At this moment the camera moves to focus in on the gracefully thin, long-limbed nude statue. The limbless statue appears behind Guy again when his newly pregnant wife confronts him about "not looking at me," and it is also shown when he hesitates to touch Rosemary's stomach after she jubilantly announces, "It's alive!"

The fears of sexuality and pregnancy that Guy may also harbor are in keeping with generalized social attitudes. Once Rosemary becomes pregnant, everyone begins to treat her strangely. The exaggerated fussing of the Castevets and of her friends at the party she gives is complemented by her husband's attitude of fear and avoidance. All convince her that her body has become an object of special consideration, for she is treated more as a pregnancy than as a person. Such a response contains components of sexual inhibition similar to the those embedded in the solicitous cluckings of Minnie and Laura-Louise when Rosemary earlier announces that she is menstruating. These attitudes form the background of her paranoia, and the audience responds to them as unremarkable because we are part of the same culture.

Yet social attitudes per se are not at issue here so much as the more global worldview implied by religious conviction. Polanski's *Rosemary's Baby* speaks to the ludicrous nature of all religious beliefs, for all religions grant the world an unambiguous meaning that the film wants to deny it. The book, by contrast, unambiguously accepts the reality of devils—and of God.

The most striking difference between the film and the novel is the way in which the supernatural motif is handled. While Levin's story ultimately takes the question of the existence of God and the devil seriously, Polanski relentlessly satirizes it throughout the film by equating good with evil. Rosemary's uneasy agnosticism, an important theme in the book, is glossed over in the film, which includes a shot of a *Time* magazine cover announcing, "God Is Dead." As several critics have noted, the movie's final scene, with Rosemary in madonnalike attire receiving a foreigner bringing gifts, explicitly parodies the birth of Christ.[38] Earlier, during the dinner Rosemary and Guy share with their friend Hutch, Polanski adds a ghoulish joke about the Agnus Dei of Christian mythology: "They cooked and ate several young children, including a niece," observes Hutch, describing the activities of the infamous Trench sisters, who formerly occupied the Bramford. Meanwhile, he serves the lamb he has just taken from the oven while his guests sip wine. The witches' cannibalism is thereby casually equated with Christian ritual. The conversation continues with Hutch's comment, "In 1959 a dead infant was found wrapped in a newspaper in the basement." To which Guy responds, "Mmm—you really rouse my appetite." "Drink your wine," Hutch replies. Such equations of orthodox religion with profane sects suggest that all religious beliefs are characterized by the projection of dark impulses that exist within their devotees.

If such dark impulses may motivate Rosemary's growing "faith" in a cult, they may also motivate the audience's desire to reach a similar point of certainty within the slippery world of the film. For Polanski calls all belief into question by continually playing tricks with the film's illusion of reality.[39] On the one hand, he repeatedly flaunts its verisimilitude. It is clear, for instance, that Mia Farrow actually has blood drawn from her arm in the scene in which Rosemary first visits the obstetrician Dr. Hill. At the same time, however, the meaning of the most naturalistic images is continually called into question. Half-open doorways suggest a hidden reality by the partial views they offer of what is happening behind them, for people and actions are often only half seen. Rosemary's actor-husband, Guy, clearly shows her both of his shoulders as in the novel to prove he has not been marked by the witches. But Rosemary looks dissatisfied at this revelation and does not respond, "All right," as she does in the book. Such ambiguities leave the audience with no conclusive sense of the nature of the reality the film is depicting.

Similar ambiguities are invoked by the casting of minor parts. The seemingly trustworthy Dr. Hill is played by Charles Grodin, whose too-even voice and manner would type him in later roles as a duplicitous opportunist. Elisha Cook, familiar to moviegoers as a small-time hood, has here been transformed into Mr. Niklas, a prim building superintendent. Conversely, Ralph Bellamy, long known for portrayals of bland but honest businessmen, has become a sinister, bearded Jewish physician. Though all of these performers play their roles creditably, the audience remains vaguely uneasy about them.

Sound gradually becomes ambiguous as well. An unexplained crashing sound interrupts Rosemary's conversation with her neighbor in the building's laundry room. As in the book, the heroine ascribes sinister overtones to the event. Earlier, during Rosemary and Guy's first evening together in their new living quarters, the expected sound of the traffic and of a plane overhead are interrupted by another more inexplicable sound of chanting. Guy's joking remark, "Shhh . . . I think I hear the Trench sisters chewing," relegates the strange noises in the old building to supernatural causes, lightly invoking a level of explanation that Rosemary will take more seriously as she becomes more and more obsessed with the peculiar sounds she hears from the Castevets' apartment.

The meaning of words can also be treacherous. Mr. Nicklas's protest, "No, no, no, no, not in the apartment!" is a case in point. And later, when Rosemary's friend Hutch remarks that World War II brought tenants back to the notorious Bramford, Rosemary's subsequent exclamation, "Terrific!" prompts him to inquire, "What? The house?"—to which she responds, "No, the lamb." Such misunderstandings suggest the difficulty of interpreting language. Similar ambiguities arise as Rosemary later attempts to decipher the anagram that holds the key to the diabolical plot against her by means of a Scrabble set. For in Polanski's film the most plausible explanation of linguistic meanings is not necessarily the correct one.

Polanski's camera lingers over such ambiguities in order to emphasize their inherently irresolvable nature. Hence, until Rosemary finally draws an irrevocable conclusion about her surroundings, the pacing is slow.[40] At moments of great stress, such as when the coven enters the apartment and when she wakes after having given birth, we even hear clocks ticking.

What may finally be accepted as plausible may, in fact, be only what serves the interests of the psyche. Accordingly, changes in the environment echo the stages of Rosemary's regression. As her sense of security ebbs away, the filmic effects increasingly emphasize a threatened and polarized vision of the world. The paternal intimacy of Hutch's apartment gives way to an *Alice-in-Wonderland* vastness when Rosemary and Guy are in their own apartment, the result of the wide-angle perspectives viewed from camera positions near the floor. The distorting and intimidating effect of wide-angle photography is even more pronounced near the end of the film when a hand-held camera precedes the fleeing Rosemary down the cavernous passages to the safety of her apartment. Similarly, the sweet harmonies of the film's opening lullaby are eventually replaced by dissonances that dramatize both Rosemary's pain and the diabolical machinations she perceives around her. And the film's color at first contrasts the foreboding darkness of the elderly Mrs. Gardinia and Hutch's apartments with the bright primary hues of the youthful Rosemary and Guy. Soon, however, this transformation leads to the garish discordances of the Castevets and ultimately to the devastating conflagrations depicted in their painting of a burning church.

The film's conclusion, in which the coven is revealed as an actuality, allows the audience to escape confronting these disturbing intimations of infantile psychological states. In a deeper way, however, Polanski decisively implicates us in such states through his naturalized portrayal of a fantastic world. For it is finally that dimension of the film that frightens us. By involving us with a seemingly normal character in a seemingly normal world, *Rosemary's Baby* gradually takes not only its heroine but also its audience back to a time of powerlessness and of traumatic confusion between fantasy and reality. Though we never see Rosemary's baby, the last image of Rosemary herself superimposes its unnatural eyes over her own; for the alien forces that terrorize her ultimately arise from within herself. The spectator's involvement with her is an involvement with these internal forces. To leave Polanski's film confident of its outcome is thus to deny the nature of our participation in it. The horror generated by *Rosemary's Baby* is finally a horror of the helpless infancy we all once suffered.

The Body as Theater:
The Tenant

The Tenant represents Polanski's most radical attempt to blend the realistic techniques of the popular horror films and the fragmented antiforms of his more personal, modernist work. Like *Repulsion* and *Rosemary's Baby*, it plays on the ambiguities between real conspiracy and paranoid delusion. But, if *Rosemary's Baby's* reliance upon a supernatural explanation effects a false closure, *The Tenant*, like *Repulsion*, betrays the ambiguity by simply, at the end, revealing its protagonist as insane.[41] This dilemma is inherent in Roland Topor's novel, which Polanski and Gerard Brach closely adapted for the screen.

As in his other exercises in horror, Polanski initially encourages us to empathize with his hero, Trelkovsky, a young Polish clerk trying to find an apartment in overcrowded Paris. But as the narrative proceeds, Trelkovsky becomes increasingly schizophrenic. Audiences have a difficult time accepting this shift, in part because of the particular nature of the insanity that is portrayed. Trelkovsky's illness, unlike Carol's in *Repulsion*, contains strong elements of hebephrenia, which is marked by silliness and exaggerated mimicry of others (in this case, primarily mimicry of Simone Choule, the former tenant of the apartment he rents). Manifestations of such behavior are disconcerting when encountered in everyday life, and they tend to become even more repellent when magnified on the screen in the person of a character toward whom we initially feel sympathetic.

An even greater problem for audiences, however, is that *The Tenant*, as it mirrors its protagonist's breakdown, abandons the realistic conventions established at the beginning of the film. As in *Repulsion*, but even more radically, suspense and logical narrative flow are eventually almost entirely abandoned in favor of a technique that emphasizes the confusion of reality and fantasy. The film indulges in distorted caricature to render Trelkovsky's hatred and fear. The story line is often motivated by the logic of the hero's emotional projections rather than by any objective sequence or relationships. These techniques make it difficult to follow the development of the most simple elements of plot in *The Tenant*. Yet the film's action does develop in such a way that the protagonist's increasingly regressive patterns of perception are echoed in the world around him. Consequently, an understanding of the obscure plot is essential to an understanding of the character's paranoid psychology and the film's aesthetic.

Polanski's initial tracking shot mimics the consolidating tendencies of such paranoid constructions. The extended camera movement begins with a medium shot of Trelkovsky's window, moving down and around to reveal a long view of the courtyard of his new apartment building before concluding on a close shot of the protagonist as he approaches the door of the concierge. The seamless connectedness of things outside the self is thus emphasized: too solid to be attacked, they are seen as monstrously encroaching on Trelkovsky's psyche, which will eventually become his sole arena of activity. By contrast, a montage of disassociated close-ups opens *Repulsion,* which deals with catatonia and murder rather than paranoia and suicide. For Carol, unlike Trelkovsky, sees the world as fragments, and to destroy a fragment that seems to her to be threatening becomes an acceptable means of attaining safety. Trelkovsky, however, recognizes no such options; he is more and more thrown back into himself.

In the realistic beginning of the film, Trelkovsky (played by Polanski himself) is intent on conforming.[42] His clothes are tasteful and drab. When the ill-tempered dog belonging to the concierge snaps at him, he responds, "Nice little doggie," and asks its name. He attempts to mollify the other tenants in his building by preserving an exaggeratedly quiet and polite demeanor. He even makes an effort to respond sexually to women, although the two he has any relations with have offensive qualities: one is grossly obese, and even Simone's friend, the motherly Stella, paints her fingernails a repulsive shade of green and enjoys the erotic stimulation of kung fu films.

Trelkovsky is disgusted by the notion of sexual intimacy, as he is by anything having to do with his body. He is excessively prudish. When he must excuse himself to use the men's room, he offers an elaborate explanation involving a nonexistent telephone call. He is plagued by his garbage, which contains unpleasant remnants of food he has consumed; and his sense of unease about his neighbors gradually focuses on their activities in the building's water closet, which is visible from his window.

From his perspective, all bodies appear repulsive. His fellow tenants are old and ugly. Even more repulsive are the elderly patients at the hospital in which he visits Simone just before she dies from a suicide attempt. At Simone's funeral, he hears a sermon, which he reimagines in accordance with his obsessions. "The worms shall consume thy eyes, thy lips, thy mouth," the priest chants, caressing his own mouth obscenely as he speaks. "They shall enter into my ears, they shall enter into my nostrils. My body shall putrify into its inmost recesses. And I shall give off a noisome stench."

In part as a consequence of this hallucinatory admonition, Trelkovsky begins to be haunted by images of fragmented body parts that echo his rapidly disintegrating sense of his own physical integrity: a tooth buried in the wall, a head bouncing in the courtyard, plaster busts of women on people's mantels, a little girl with her leg in a brace. He feels increasingly uncertain about the unity of his own body. "At what precise moment does an individual cease to be the person he—and everyone else—believes him to be," he mutters to himself. "If one severs an arm, one says, 'myself and my arm.' But what if one's head is amputated? Is it then 'myself and my body?' By what right does the head claim the title of myself?" As he indulges in these musings, his passivity becomes complete, and he allows Stella to undress him as if he were a baby.

As he loses his sense of identification with his own body, Simone Choule's takes its place. Trelkovsky is certain that Simone's body must be more desirable, more acceptable, than his own. She is the one to whom others are constantly comparing him, always to his detriment. It is she who is really part of the space he is presently usurping: her clothes are in the closet, her tooth in the wall.

Besides, she is a woman, and he carries his maleness uneasily. He is not as powerful, as virile as others of his own sex. When a coworker urges him to stand up to his neighbors, he cringes in terror as the man marches aggressively around the room with a beer bottle held defiantly up to his mouth. His landlord carries a long loaf of French bread under his arm as he suavely persuades the timid clerk not to report the robbery of his apartment to the police. In Trelkovsky's view, there is only one conclusion to be drawn: if being a man involves asserting oneself and thereby risking exposing oneself, it is better to don a false mask of womanhood.[43]

The beginnings of his transformation occur during a brief illness, when his sense of physical well-being is eroded to a fatal degree. From the water closet, he looks across to his own apartment and finds that he is gazing at his own image in the window. This marks the onset of his psychosis, the irredeemable split between himself and his body.

When, unable to tolerate the reality of his own body, Trelkovsky adopts that of Simone, he confronts facets of her identity that further exacerbate his own obsessions. Simone has been an Egyptologist, and her form first appears encased in mummylike bandages. Thus, in addition to her association with the death and putrefaction toward which Trelkovsky finds himself inextricably drawn, she symbolizes a threatening oriental otherness. Through the willful destruction of her body, Simone has found a way to express a virulent loathing of her physical being. Trelkovsky, also despising his body, envies her courage. Ultimately, his own body, as if independent of his real self, becomes a caricature of Simone, grotesquely mimicking her final, suicidal leap from the apartment window to the greenhouse below. The dogged insistence on mechanical repetition that characterizes extreme psychotic rigidity forces him up the stairs a second time to conduct yet another performance of her most dramatic moment. Meanwhile, his inner self, horrified and alienated, has by this point been reduced to the role of a passive and helpless observer of the macabre antics of this false physical self. He has become the tenant of his own body.[44]

In its role as observer, Trelkovsky's inner self is analogous to Polanski's audience, which also bears passive witness to a performance that becomes increasingly grotesque and unreal: the action of the film itself. Trelkovsky's

Polanski, as the title character of The Tenant, *gazes fearfully out into the courtyard of his building. Courtesy of the* Chicago Reader.

false self, his visible persona in the film, can be seen as the false self of the audience; for, like Trelkovsky's inner self, we watch and judge from a privileged, disembodied position as the character interacts with his environment.

At first we sympathize with Trelkovsky's outer self, persuaded by Polanski's portrayal of plausible causes for the protagonist's morbid attitude. His surroundings are dull, almost colorless; and Phillippe Sarde's music, featuring a single oboe and cello, establishes a melancholy mood. As a foreigner in an unfriendly country, he feels like an unwelcome tenant wherever he goes. His officemates and the concierge of his building are loud and vulgar. His landlord is imperious; the other tenants are cold and self-righteous. People seem willfully unpleasant; perhaps there is a plot against him.

But this empathic construction, so consonant with the conventions of realism, is undercut as the world of the false self grows more eccentric and incredible. Small sounds such as the dripping of a faucet become exaggerated. People begin to appear as unreal caricatures; and their voices seem increasingly disconnected from their bodies, a result of the director's manipulation of the film's postsynchronized dubbing procedures.[45] Simone Choule herself first appears as an almost ludicrous cliché from the horror tradition represented by *The Mummy*.[46] The growing confusion between the false self and the environment is revealed through distorted images of Trelkovsky's apartment, where space contracts and expands in accordance with his mood. Events now appear contradictory and confused; for we have entered a world of fantasy and hallucination. The environment is gradually transformed into a gaudily dressed theater set, and the protagonist's actions seem pointlessly ludicrous.

Yet Polanski never allows us to forget that we are watching a movie. He characteristically makes us question the motives that underlie our interest in the false self of the filmic body he has created. Portrait shots of the protagonist and other characters are typically set within strongly defined window frames, and the film also includes numerous cinematic references. There is even a film within the film; its audience includes Trelkovsky and Stella, who engage in sexual activity while watching Bruce Lee on the screen. And there is a passive, voyeuristic observer behind them, who is content to look at behavior in others that he cannot admit to in himself. The analogy to Polanski's own audience is clear; for we too may be looking for an alternate, false self upon which to project unacceptable impulses toward sexuality and aggression that we consciously deny to our "real" selves.

Such a construction of the audience's motives is reinforced by another sequence of shots. At Simone's funeral, Trelkovsky's interest in Stella, who is sitting nearby, is repressed when he notices a little girl observing him. This observing presence triggers his fantasy about a funeral sermon centering on his disgust with his body, and finally causes him to flee the church in terror. Unlike the patron at the kung fu movie, the little girl has no discernible reason for looking other than innocent curiosity. But to Trelkovsky she is feminine innocence penetrating his inner self and discovering carnal desires there. She may, in fact, be herself a fantasy, a projection of Trelkovsky's guilt, since another tenant later identifies the same child as a boy.

Later Trelkovsky discovers that the child's mother, another foreigner, is, or imagines herself to be, a victim of persecutory action by the other tenants. When Trelkovsky's metamorphosis into Simone is complete, he hallucinates a scene in which mother and daughter are in the courtyard being beaten by his neighbors. The neighbors place a red cloak and jester's cap on the child and also a mask of Trelkovsky. Thus attired, the little girl points up to his window and, seeing Trelkovsky's own anomalous costume, jeers. In this way, the victimized become victimizers, revenging themselves by looking without empathy, ridiculing what they see rather than sympathizing with it. This attack on the audience also includes the director himself. The mask of Trelkovsky the child wears is also a mask of Polanski, for whom the film also represents a false self, a vicarious playing out of perverse desires. But falsity and unreality are everywhere by now: in the false self of Trelkovsky, in the detached pose of the director, and in the "innocent" voyeurism of the audience. This multiple splitting signals a level of psychosis in which the inner self becomes further fragmented, empty, and at war within itself. At this stage, the audience, too, is made into a false self. Near the end of the film Polanski's camera tracks around the building's courtyard again, which the beleaguered hero now sees as a fantastic, theatrically decorated arena for entertainment. It is peopled by the other tenants, a viciously caricatured audience, who applaud and cheer Trelkovsky on as he prepares to jump from his window.

In this film, Polanski pushes his attack on the audience to an extreme where it feels forced and excessive, for we have felt more for Trelkovsky than mere curiosity and sadistic voyeurism. We have felt empathy—because the film's realist conventions initially asked it of us. And we may feel betrayed by the director's radical shift of modes, a shift which attempts to deny the meaningfulness of our original relationship to the narrative. The problem, however, may not lie simply with Polanski's film but with the horror genre itself. Polanski, with his usual contrariety, has forced the audience to face up to the squalid nature of our pleasure in the genre even as he has satisfied it.

In contrast to the modernist films, which inspire ennui through their static forms, *The Tenant* tries to effect too radical a shift in its narrative modes. Beginning with a realistic presumption about the effect of a xenophobic society on an outsider, it moves into bizarre and fragmented depictions of extreme mental disorder. To some extent, all of his horror films face similar problems in relation to their endings. For how is it possible to resolve a story that gradually creates greater and greater ambiguities about the nature of reality? *Rosemary's Baby* and *Dance of the Vampires* effect closure at one level by understanding the protagonists' problems in terms of plots perpetrated against them. *Repulsion* takes the opposite tack, pulling us back from a heroine it defines as insane. More than any of the other horror films, however, *The Tenant* tries to sustain its ambiguity to the end by portraying ever more regressed views both of its hero and of the world around him. But the audience may finally draw back from the film's excesses, for what originally inspired empathy through plausibility and coherence becomes alienating through its grotesquerie.

In *The Tenant*, Polanski pushes the psychology of the horror story to its limit. As in his modernist projects, he has reached a cul-de-sac. Fortunately, however, his career has taken him in still other directions. In *Macbeth* he encountered history, both the political history the play describes and the historicity of the play itself. The developing psychological processes he explored in the horror films are thus balanced by a depiction of social and political processes.

4

History as Nightmare: *Macbeth*

HAVING EXPLORED MODERNISM and the horror story, Polanski turned his attention in 1971 to a backward look at the great traditions of Western culture. There were personal as well as aesthetic reasons for this decision. Two years earlier, his pregnant wife and three of his friends had been senselessly murdered by a cult led by Charles Manson. The experience spurred the director to look beyond the decadence of contemporary culture for material that could inspire him in new ways. "After the murders, everything seemed futile to me," he later recalled. "I couldn't think of a subject that seemed worthwhile or dignified enough to spend a year or more on it, in view of what had happened to me."[1]

His background predisposed him toward *Macbeth*. As an admirer of the films of Orson Welles and Laurence Olivier, he understandably thought of adapting Shakespeare. "As a kid, I loved Shakespeare, and when I was a teenager I saw Laurence Olivier's *Hamlet* twenty times. I always had a great desire to make a Shakespearean movie."[2] Surrealist painter Salvador Dali had illustrated a published version of *Macbeth*, to which Polanski pays direct homage in his images of the three weird sisters and the sleepy grooms. And the drama's affinity with an absurdist outlook is attested to by the fact that Eugene Ionesco was at the time working on his own adaptation of Shakespeare's text, *Macbett*.

Polanski's filmmaking instincts also led him to the play. He has said that he chose *Macbeth* "because there are a lot of lines and descriptions that are verbal but can be easily translated into great action scenes and because there is a great character in Macbeth who can be developed and shown in a new way on the screen."[3] In addition, the motifs of brutality and witchcraft suited his state, and, most importantly, the theme of sexual enslavement could be integrated into the portrayal of the hero without doing too much violence to the original text.

The timing of the film and the circumstances of its production colored many of the initial reviews. It was Polanski's first effort following his wife's gruesome death and the first movie financed by Playboy Enterprises. As such, its violence and sexuality were often seen as extrinsic to its artistic

purpose. Moreover, many critics were outraged over the lack of respect
shown to Shakespeare's text. In response to such objections, Polanski emphasized the historical authenticity of his film. He frequently mentioned
that he had cowritten the script with British author-critic Kenneth Tynan,
a former literary director of the British National Theatre. "Whatever I did
in the film," Polanski insisted, "I based on different research and on different opinions of scholars."[4] He even defended his unorthodox ending in
these terms. "As a matter of fact, the way I ended the film was a part of
history," he said. "Donalbain later became king. . . . The ending is the
way it seems to me in Shakespeare."[5]

In a similar spirit, Polanski shot *Macbeth* on location in Britain, using
Snowdonia National Park in Wales for exteriors, Bamburgh Castle in
Northumberland as Dunsinane, and Linisfarne Castle on Holy Island (the
location of *Cul-de-Sac*) for Inverness. The production designer, Wilfred
Shingleton, has described the elaborate efforts that were made to achieve
a feeling of accuracy in the castle sets. Extensive reconstruction work was
done, in which part of the aim was to create "a feeling of construction in
the images—to make it look as though the castles were in a constant state
of being built."[6]

Polanski's meticulousness caused problems: shooting took twenty-five
weeks—ten weeks longer than had been anticipated—and the $2.4 mil-
lion budget was exceeded by $600,000. Nonetheless, the director had
achieved the effect of accuracy he wanted, although it was not an accuracy
designed to satisfy the objections of many Shakespeareans, who were upset over Polanski's tendency to play down the verbal dimension of the
original text. In an article entitled "Shakespeare in the Movies," Frank
Kermode wrote: "The film we see mustn't spoil [Shakespeare's] astonish-
ing effects of language. In Polanski's film, these are lost."[7] By contrast,
Polanski himself saw the problem as one of translating the play's meaning
into visual terms. "We always took the explanation that was the most visual, that was the most useful for our cinematographic adaptation," he has
said of the process he and Tynan went through in order to arrive at a specific interpretation of the play. "I also tried to translate into a visual whatever was possible to translate."[8] Such translations contributed to the
elimination of a third of the play's language.

This emphasis on visualization led Polanski to show many of the scenes
that Shakespeare had chosen to create solely through words, including the
murder of Duncan. "If you make a film about a murder," the director
claims, "you have to *show* the murder, or do a film about something else.
If you use the screen as a medium, then what you tell has to be told by
visual means. Of course, you could put a guy in front of a camera and have
him read the play and the same story would be told to your audience in a
different, perhaps more gentle way. I happen to think it would also be a
more boring way."[9]

Thus the film substitutes a visual poetry of violence for Shakespeare's verbal one, resulting in a version that, as one critic has observed, "cuts the rhythm of the play with bear-baiting [and] scenes of carnage," while "the major soliloquies are not delivered as major determinants of the action, but in an offhand manner, as asides."[10] Polanski's emphasis on the visual does not, in fact, forgo the psychological complexity communicated by Shakespeare's soliloquies, but rather expresses this complexity more through the choice and handling of the images than through reverence to Shakespeare's language. Many critics felt that this approach constituted what Stanley Kauffmann called "a straight, serious attempt to make the play a film."[11]

The objection of one commentator that the "living ambiguity" of the play had been lost was valid in the sense that the director built his drama around a particular reading of the play that owes much to the absurdist one put forward by Polish critic Jan Kott.[12] Kott writes, "Unlike Shakespeare's historical plays, *Macbeth* does not show history as the Grand Mechanism. It shows it as a nightmare. History, shown as a mechanism, fascinates by its very terror and inevitability. Whereas nightmare paralyses and terrifies."[13] From this perspective, Macbeth's progress represents his gradual realization of this terror. "He can accept himself at last," according to Kott, "because he has realized that every choice is absurd, or rather, that there is no choice."[14]

The Psychology of Nightmare

For Polanski the nightmare is more psychological than political. *Macbeth* follows the pattern of the horror films by focusing on the internal experience of its protagonist. His realistic style again stretches to include the hallucinatory imagery of dreams and visions as well as the grotesque distortion of objects that characterize the other films in this group. And Polanski encourages us to see the events he portrays as projections of his hero's mental state by repeatedly showing Macbeth watching the action in profile at the side of the screen and by presenting his soliloquies in part as the voice-over narration of an authorial presence. Each stage of the hero's psychological deterioration is connected with recurring series of motifs and images.

Like Rosemary, Trelkovsky, and Carol, Polanski's Macbeth is searching for a mature identity. And, like them, his inability to achieve this goal is the result of internal conflicts related to a troubled sexuality. The director therefore portrays his hero and heroine as young people, even at times childish, though this feature differentiates them from the image many critics hold of Shakespeare's characters.

Through the first parts of the film Macbeth moves back and forth between two worlds. We first see him as part of a grim milieu of male brutality. He gains respite from this bloody world by returning to his castle, which initially appears to us as a vision in a fairytale, and to his wife, who, with her fair hair and sky-blue gown, seems the ideal princess to inhabit this haven. The opposition between Macbeth's sentimental romanticism and the true significance of his homelife emerges only gradually. We are introduced to Lady Macbeth as she is stroking her dogs; and later when she shrieks with delight as the dogs set upon a shackled bear we begin to recognize the amoral perversity behind her facade of childish high spirits. She unleashes her enthralled husband on Duncan with an equal lack of compunction. To her, regicide seems just another adventure, and she cajoles and whimpers until it is accomplished. Earlier she dances unconcernedly with their intended victim and allows him to kiss her, tacitly reminding Macbeth that her affection is a prize to be bestowed on whomever she deems most worthy.[15] Though she represents something opposed to male warfare, it is neither benign nor mature.

Macbeth will do anything to insure the love of this woman, but ironically she insists upon a proof of his devotion that will alienate him from her irrevocably: regicide. After he has murdered the king, Macbeth cannot bring himself to touch his wife; and afterwards we see them lying silently next to one another in bed. Later, as Lady Macbeth sobs brokenly to herself over what has happened, she bears a striking resemblance to one of the weird sisters, whose visible nudity has already documented their sexual repulsiveness. And still later, in the sleepwalking scene, Lady Macbeth herself appears nude, and the absence of erotic charge in the display suggests the indifference her husband has come to feel for her. (Ironically, this very absence of eroticism led many of the film's early reviewers to praise the "tastefulness" of Polanski's use of nudity.)

Failing in his attempt to establish a mature sexual rapport with his wife, Macbeth turns back to the world of males. Now, though women may surround him, he dreams only of men. In this world he finds appearances equally deceptive. But here erotic impulses are masked by violence. Macbeth's murder of Duncan is shown in terms of sexual perversity. Gently pulling back the coverlet to reveal the King's nakedness, Macbeth kneels astride his victim and stabs him repeatedly. Later, in the witches' womblike cave, he has visions of Fleance and Banquo and of Malcolm and Donalbain mocking him. After he has claimed the crown as his own, he dreams that Fleance snatches it from him in a similarly sexual manner, again preceding the act of taking the crown by pulling back the coverlet.

His growing sense of psychic unease focuses more and more on his own body. Accordingly, emotionally charged images of ingestion abound. At the banquet preceding Duncan's murder he is unable to eat, though his wife gobbles her food voraciously. But after he has given in to his libidinous and violent yearning for the crown, he devours meat carelessly, and

A broken Lady Macbeth is cared for by her nurse. Courtesy of the Film Stills Archive, The Museum of Modern Art, New York.

when the weird sisters offer him their disgusting brew, he gulps it down as though welcoming its corrupting potency.

His inner state of disordered desire is also rendered by the prevalence of images of physical mutilation and fragmentation. In his dream an armored figure appears, but it has no body to support it and it crumbles pathetically; a snake crawls out of its vacant helmet. During the final battle sequence Macbeth is particularly effective in creating ruin, stabbing one adversary in the throat, another in the face, a third in the groin. Meanwhile, the corpse of his dead wife lies pitifully mangled in the courtyard below, only partly covered by a carelessly thrown blanket.

This pathetic image of Lady Macbeth emphasizes what her husband is all too conscious of: the fragility of the human body. His fears about his own physical being center on the tenuous connection between the body proper and the head. Macbeth first appears with three hanging men in the background; and shortly afterward we witness the first Thane of Cawdor executed by means of an iron collar placed around his neck. As Macbeth becomes increasingly incapable of identifying himself with his body as a whole, he grows ever more concerned about his head alone. His slow, clumsy movements during the final battle with Macduff are juxtaposed to the possessiveness he feels about his crown, which first assumes this exaggerated significance during his murder of Duncan. When Macduff offers him an option, he chooses to keep the crown rather than regain his sword; it is as if he felt that he would die without it. Finally decapitated, he is literally reduced to a head.

The battle preceding this catastrophe is played as an infantile fantasy in which the world behaves in accordance with Macbeth's own wishes and fears. He first appears tiny and alone on his throne at the end of a cavernous vista. But his belief in his own inviolability is magical. Effortlessly, he kills all the soldiers who surround him. He even has it in his power to kill Macduff until his mistake in trusting the witches' deceptive rhetoric undermines his confidence. Then his superhuman command of the situation vanishes. With the shattering of this last, childishly charmed mode of controlling the life around him, he abruptly becomes vulnerable and is soon dismembered. The image of the trunkless head is particularly pathetic after the athletic prowess we have just seen. And when the cycle begins again at the cave of the weird sisters, it is with a hero whose body is already maimed at the outset. The nightmare of regression is thus presented as an endlessly recurring one.

The Regressive Pattern of History

Though much of the force of Polanski's film derives from its powerful expression of Macbeth's regression, the nightmarish quality of the film transcends the purely psychological. By choosing this play as his subject, Polanski was forced to formulate an approach to social and political processes, as they develop over time, which he had never before had to confront. His solution involved placing these phenomena within the context of a hostile, chaotic cosmos—a nightmare world. As far as possible, he also flattened the ebb and flow of historical pattern by making the state into an entity eternally reproducing horror and corruption. But some acknowledgment of historical change was inevitable, even if it only involved the worsening of what was abhorrent to begin with. Such a vision informs Polanski's film, expanding his earlier preoccupation with psychological regression to the social sphere.

Polanski's *Macbeth* takes place in a world where magic reigns in the place of rationality. Humankind is at the mercy of forces it can neither understand nor control. In such a world, there is no virtue but merely the attempt to avoid evil. The film both begins and ends with the three witches, who initially carry out their prognosticative rites (burying a noose and a dismembered arm clutching a knife) on the desolate beach that will soon see Duncan claiming victory following a bloody battle. At the film's conclusion, Duncan's younger son, too, falls under their spell, arriving at their lair during an oppressive downpour. There are many such downpours in the film. In place of the dramatic changes between fair and foul in the play, Polanski offers gray skies, drizzle, and mud. Nothing is cheerful for long. Our first vision is of a breathtakingly beautiful beach at sunrise, engagingly impressionistic in its soft pastels and delicate play of light. Then, as we look at it, the beach changes before our eyes into something gloomy, stern, and unyielding. Halfway through the film, we see a bolder play of color as the soldiers in Malcolm's English camp perform their maneuvers. But this display, too, quickly gives way to mud and dinginess as Macduff is told about the slaughter of his family. A similar impression of vividness occurs again near the film's end as the army assumes its formation before Dunsinane. But again, the invitation proves chimerical as the colors fade into the cold, gray stone of the castle and the dull silver armor of Macbeth and his antagonists.

What can Macbeth hope to attain in such a universe? Here there are no divine kings with gifts of prophecy and healing, as in Shakespeare's text. Instead we find barbaric and callous warlords with weak, corruptible heirs. Duncan first appears immediately after one of his vassals has efficiently bludgeoned a still-stirring corpse lying on the battlefield. Soon afterward, he oversees the execution of the first Thane of Cawdor, who must leap from a parapet so that his neck may be broken by means of an iron collar that has been chained to it.

Yet Duncan at least seems strong and honest, while his sons appear to be neither. Malcolm stutters uncertainly at times, and his reaction to Cawdor's execution is to speak Shakespeare's line "Nothing became his life like the leaving of it" almost as though it were a question. All of his major speeches have been cut, including the crucial one affirming the restoration of order and health to the state at the play's conclusion. Instead, the film concludes on an image of the shifty-faced, club-footed Donalbain, already plotting to overthrow his elder sibling.

Through such visual stereotyping, Polanski invites us to judge by appearances; but appearances are also deceptive. Ross, who has the face of a cherub, is the greatest villain of all in this version of the story. His sole ambition is to be Thane of Cawdor, and for this he is willing to do anything. We first see him guarding the former Thane, whose blood-smeared body is lashed to a sledge on the battlefield. When the king hears the news of his vassal's treachery, he entrusts the Thane's necklace to Ross so that the latter may serve as an emissary to bestow it upon Macbeth. This necklace henceforth serves as the emblem of Ross's ambition, much as the crown does for Macbeth's. To obtain it, the nobleman is willing to do anything: engineer the murder of Macduff's family, participate in that of Banquo. Macbeth, however, continues to overlook Ross, eventually placing the Thane's necklace around the throat of another vassal who has presum-

Macbeth and Banquo amid the grim surroundings of their battle encampment. Courtesy of the Film Stills Archive, The Museum of Modern Art, New York.

ably compromised himself far less in his lord's service. Despairing of a just reward for his unjust activities, Ross abandons the Scottish ship of state to take refuge with what he calculates to be the winning side. At the end, it is he, bland and smiling, who places the crown on Malcolm's head.

Ross, while not representative of all minions of the state, has nevertheless outwitted the best. Macduff, by contrast, is truly virtuous. His nobility of character is, however, concealed behind a perpetual five-o'clock shadow and a vaguely dull-witted expression. His undisclosed reasons for leaving his wife and family are defended by Ross—in this version, hardly an apologist who inspires belief. Later Macduff is informed of the calamity that has resulted from his ill-considered retreat by the very perpetrator of the debacle.

So, though Macduff ultimately triumphs over Macbeth, and though Malcolm ultimately becomes king, little has changed, for Ross continues, apparently ready to serve this ruler with the same unscrupulous zeal with which he has served the last—and the one before. If Duncan stood at the head of a more orderly kingdom than Macbeth, it was not a better one; for he, too, relied on Ross. Though the nightmare may worsen, it was a nightmare from the beginning.

On at least two occasions, Polanski conveys this sense of inescapable menace through extraordinarily long takes of highly complex mise-en-scènes. In the first, Macduff comes to waken the just-murdered Duncan, and the camera moves purposefully around the courtyard as various characters enter, speak their lines, and leave. The state of confusion here documented is also imitated, as the camera's relentless linking of the remaining major characters mimics their own attempts to establish a new order. To achieve this goal, they must first find a culprit to whom they can attach the regicide so that they can safely recognize a new priority of leadership. The camera, however, denies these possibilities by finishing its track on the unstable image of the staircase and the balcony around which the characters are grouped in shifting and uneasy patterns. Macduff, standing below, registers an amazement similar to that of the others as Macbeth, on reentering from the balcony, announces that he has murdered the grooms. But the former's incredulous question—"Wherefore did you do so?"—lacks authority. Standing below, Macduff can only offer weak, tentative resistance—though later, in the battle sequence, he will follow Macbeth up a stairway and onto the more stable space of a balcony in order to decapitate him, this time with the strength of the English force behind him.

Such uncertainties become even more disturbing during another long take of Ross telling Macduff about his family's slaughter. The camera follows the two Scottish noblemen as they wander among the troops preparing for battle, and in the midst of all this organized activity Macduff appears as a hopelessly naive sentimentalist, casually duped by the Machiavellian Ross, the very man against whom the major part of his wrath should properly be directed. But, even though the audience enjoys a position of superior understanding here, it is not a secure one. For just as Ross dupes Macduff with an "objective" representation of events, so may we be duped by Polanski. The very virtuosity of the complexly realistic mise-en-scène raises subliminal suspicions about the ability of the film itself to "take us in."

In such carefully orchestrated scenes, the effect of deep space feels strained and subtly "plotted." Wilfred Shingleton's sets contain similarly ominous overtones, enhancing the suspense by encompassing several different—and possibly ominous—points of view within a single frame. "When Macbeth and Lady Macbeth are talking about the killing of the King, we put them in the foreground and through the window in the background we can see the King in bed," Shingleton has recalled.[16] Shortly afterward, another set helps to sustain another kind of tension. According to Shingleton, "the high level gallery around the courtyard was designed because when Lady Macbeth goes with the sleeping potion in the pitcher to the king's room Banquo comes out with his son and walks across the courtyard. Polanski wanted to build up suspense as the audience is wondering if Banquo is going to see Lady Macbeth."[17] Here, as elsewhere, characters within the same frame are endangered by their partial perceptions of reality. Though Shingleton's sets permit the spectators to see more, our vision is also "framed." Thus we may feel equally vulnerable to such victimization.

By such means Polanski subtly taunts his audience not only about our desire to see but also about the perverse motives behind it. The image of the window through which we watch the sleeping king is picked up in other images of characters gazing out of windows. Keyholes also figure as means of viewing the action. An audience within the film is delighted by the sight of children baiting a bear. Macbeth's later comments, "I'll not be baited with the rabble's curse" and "Bearlike I must fight the course," associate him with this creature—and the audience, by implication, with the children who enjoy baiting it. Finally the hero's head is swept through a jeering "rabble" on the end of a stick. Is their pleasure like ours?

This scene, like others, is filled with impeccable period detail. But such craft operates ultimately to authenticate nothing beyond our own perverse pleasure. Polanski's monumental struggle to achieve realism in *Macbeth* thus finally raises uncertainties about reality itself. Though we witness a meticulous re-creation of history here, we experience it as a nightmare filled with chaotic and little-understood horrors. Within this nightmarish atmosphere, however, *Macbeth* explores political processes more thoroughly than any of Polanski's previous films, and this exploration was an ideal preparation for the more complex challenge of *Chinatown*.

5

The Generic Synthesis: *Chinatown*

CHINATOWN MARKS THE CULMINATION of Polanski's career. In no other film has he so successfully fused his diverse creative and cultural influences. His early years in Poland had taught him how to transform the materials of a specific culture into art. From his horror films he had learned to embed his modernist tendencies toward fragmentation and dislocation in the structure of a traditional formula. And *Macbeth* had offered him the opportunity to play off his solipsistic nihilism against a cogent vision of historical and political processes. *Chinatown* brought all of these influences into play, creating the most profoundly disturbing and purgative work of Polanski's oeuvre.

His achievement was the result not only of timing but also of circumstances. In his review of *Chinatown* Andrew Sarris argued that Polanski's gifts are enhanced through collaboration, a view the movie itself bears out. According to Sarris, "It is generally agreed that Polanski insisted on [Faye] Dunaway's death at the end of the film. By the same token, [Jack] Nicholson insisted on a subtler, less bloody rendering of a fight at the old age home. [Producer Robert] Evans vetoed Polanski's original idea for a sour, cynical absurdist score and opted instead for the romantic score now on the soundtrack."[1] In such a situation, a major part of the director's role is to synthesize the creative contributions made by a variety of talents.

The process of collaboration in this case appears to have been a difficult one. The film's original cameraman, Stanley Cortez, was, for some reason, replaced soon after the filming began.[2] In addition, the relationships between Polanski and screenwriter Robert Towne as well as that between the director and the film's female star, Faye Dunaway, were marked by well-publicized tensions that seem never to have been harmoniously resolved.[3]

In the case of Towne, Polanski saw the dispute as growing out of their different orientations to filmmaking. The director described Towne as "someone who has got a great talent for the verbal side, but none for the visual," an approach he found frustrating. "I was somehow constantly bored with the material," he commented later. "I could not have *enough*

Villain and victim: the detective-hero of Chinatown *observes neither. Courtesy of the* Chicago Reader *(top); the* Film Stills Archive, The Museum of Modern Art, *New York (bottom).*

interest in the visual side of the picture."[4] But the differences between director and screenwriter undoubtedly run even deeper. Where Towne is biased toward the romantic, commercial, and political, Polanski tends to be cynical, elitist, and antisocial. An aficionado of the hard-boiled detective genre, Towne originally envisioned a contemporary retelling of the formula as an excellent vehicle for his friend Jack Nicholson. Nicholson brought Polanski into the project only later.[5] Because of Towne, Polanski was forced to relate his thematic concerns to a context of politics and ecology. In an earlier essay on Bogart and Belmondo, Towne had expressed his admiration for the former in terms of the American star's readiness to combat fascism and his ability to commit himself to people and causes. By contrast, Towne saw the more modernist figure of Belmondo as someone to whom "nothing matters beyond him—no clash of alien ideologies, no human sufferings beyond or within his ken; only the moment."[6] A similar bias toward "commitment"—though atypical of Polanski—colors *Chinatown*. Moreover, in the character of Evelyn Mulwray, Towne created a figure of dignity and sensual warmth that goes far beyond the pathetically diminished caricatures of women that Polanski himself often favors.

The mood of romantic aspiration that surrounds this woman is enhanced by the languidly melancholy love theme composed by Hollywood veteran Jerry Goldsmith. Again the effect is achieved at the expense of Polanski's original conception. Goldsmith's score was hastily composed at the request of producer Robert Evans after a preview audience complained about the film's original music by Polanski's choice, Phillip Lambro, a distinguished modern composer who had never before worked on a film.[7] Goldsmith's tendency toward traditional Hollywood romanticism provides an unexpectedly harmonious counterpoint to the pessimistic atmosphere of decay Polanski is so adept at creating. "The music in the film is dealing with the relationship between two people," Goldsmith has said, "as well as creating a certain suspense element."[8]

Robert Evans played a pivotal role in this process of balance and accommodation between the director's modernist leanings and the more traditional approaches of his cocreators. *Chinatown* was the first film Evans had personally produced, and he appears to have devoted a considerable amount of energy and patience to arbitrating disputes and suggesting alternatives.[9] While he overruled Polanski on some issues, he supported many of the director's other unconventional ideas. Against Towne's wishes, Polanski, Evans, and production designer Richard Sylbert rewrote the script radically, changing, among other things, Towne's original ending, which featured the film's heroine, Evelyn Mulwray, murdering her father, with whom she had had an incestuous affair, to save her daughter/sister, Katherine.[10] On the whole, however, Evans's influence on Polanski was undoubtedly a restraining one. According to John Alonzo, *Chinatown's* cinematographer, "Bob Evans, as producer, had in mind a rather 'classic' type of picture."[11] And that was the approach Alonzo followed, supported by Polanski himself.

All of the director's collaborators had strong feelings for the commercial potential of their project, and the film's success rests on the way Polanski incorporated his own concerns within the realist tradition of classical Hollywood filmmaking his colleagues represented.

In keeping with this tradition, the film features complex characters, a plausible, logically coherent plot, and a socially relevant theme about corruption in city government—all expressed within the context of a well-established generic model: the private-eye story. Detective J. J. Gittes begins to investigate the illicit love life of Los Angeles Water Commissioner Hollis Mulwray only to discover that this ostensibly simple case involves both murder and high-level political tampering with the city water supply. This pattern is a familiar variation on the hard-boiled genre. *Chinatown* both exemplifies this genre and comments on it.

The Formula as Myth

Chinatown's private-eye formula has in the past been understood in realistic terms. In his celebrated private-eye manifesto *The Simple Art of Murder*, Raymond Chandler contrasted Dashiell Hammett's putative realism with the artificial contrivances of the classical detective story. As Chandler saw it, "Hammett gave murder back to the people who commit it for reasons, not just to provide a corpse; and with the means at hand, not with handwrought duelling pistols, curare, and tropical fish. He put these people down on paper as they are, and he made them talk and think in the language they customarily used for these purposes."[12] In contrast to Chandler's emphasis on realism, Polanski's version of the formula invokes nostalgia "as a means of undercutting the generic experience itself," as John Cawelti has written, and Cawelti goes on to point out that "a film like *Chinatown* deliberately evokes the basic characteristics of a traditional genre in order to bring its audience to see the genre as an embodiment of an inadequate and destructive myth."[13]

Though *Chinatown*, like its predecessors, features a milieu that is ostensibly realistic, its self-conscious visual style qualifies this assumption. In the Hollywood of the 1940s, thrillers exploited the documentary associations of black-and-white photography to create an atmosphere of gritty naturalism. *Chinatown's* ambience, by contrast, is both softer and more obviously artificial. Richard Sylbert's stylized production design, with its elegantly dated art-deco motifs, is subtly set off by Panavision framing, which provides a 1970s perspective on the mise-en-scène. John Alonzo has documented Polanski's bias toward obvious stylization. "He said to me: 'I want very much for the photography to complement the story in such a way that it will be alright if people say it is beautifully photographed, because I will bring the content up to that level.' "[14]

Color, too, tends to be used for obvious effect, as in the black, white, and red cocktail-bar scene. More generally, the colors in the film have been selected from a limited spectrum made up largely of black, white, brown, and beige. "The color tones were purposely altered for effect," Alonzo has reported. "The picture that is now in release does not look the way it looked when we shot it. The subtle brown-beige tone that it has has been added in modifying the matrices during the course of the imbibition process."[15] The costumes and sets thus appear more like elegant evocations of the spirit of a past era than like realistic re-creations of that era.

The film's characters undergo a similar modification away from the simply realistic, conforming to Artaud's notion of figures "enlarged to the stature of gods, heroes or monsters in mythic dimensions."[46] While the mannerisms of stars like Humphrey Bogart followed the acting conventions of the period so that they appeared to be behaving naturally, the performances in *Chinatown* are often contrived to appear slightly stilted. For the most part, the actors are shot in close-up. Such a technique would ordinarily intensify our empathy with them, but these characterizations are so far removed from what we conceive of as natural behavior that the close shots inspire a feeling more of awe than of easy affection.

This distanced response is most obviously evoked by John Huston, who plays the malevolent millionaire Noah Cross. Huston's real-life Hollywood background as actor and director lends a particular resonance to his deliberate and stylized depiction of a civic patriarch here. Faye Dunaway, though not the legendary figure Huston is, gives an even more stylized performance in her role as Cross's daughter Evelyn Mulwray, the femme-fatale figure required by the hard-boiled formula, and her mannerisms are complemented by the masklike makeup she wears.

In contrast to Huston and Dunaway's stilted performances, Jack Nicholson's J. J. Gittes projects an ordinariness that is almost clownish during many of the early scenes. Even while he is playing the fool, however, we are always aware of Gittes as a descendant of a legendary tradition of private-eye heroes, and our attention is drawn to Nicholson's movie-star status when Gittes's barber observes that, thanks to having his picture in the paper, he is "practically a movie star."

Polanski reinforces this mythic ambience by including specific references to the private-eye models that have shaped *Chinatown*'s narrative and thematic pattern. According to John Alonzo, Polanski was well aware of these models, being "totally informed about Raymond Chandler and Dashiell Hammett."[17] Most obviously, the presence of John Huston, director of the cinematic archetype of the hard-boiled formula, *The Maltese Falcon*, reminds us of the film's generic origins. In addition, numerous references to *The Maltese Falcon* and *The Big Sleep* have been included.

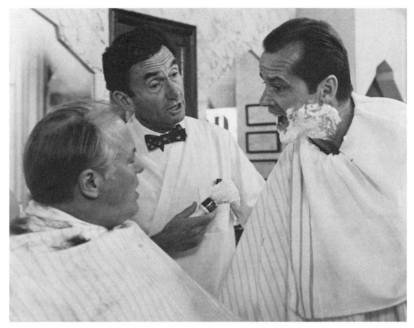

A comically attired Gittes assaults a man who has accused him of publicity-mongering after the results of his investigation have appeared on page one of the Los Angeles newspapers. Courtesy of the Chicago Reader.

A woman dressed like the *Falcon*'s Brigid O'Shaugnessey similarly gives a false name in the hero's office at the film's opening. The flirtation scene set in a cocktail bar recalls Bogart and Bacall in *The Big Sleep*. A new name is painted on an office door, but one belonging to a bureaucrat rather than to the hero as in Huston's film. Light rectangles on a wall give evidence of pictures that have been removed—again, however, they appear in the office of a bureaucrat rather than the apartment of the independent detective envisioned by Huston. Photographs of horses like those on Sam Spade's wall are scattered throughout Polanski's film. Finally, when the detective first visits the home of his wealthy client, Chandler's novel features a chauffeur polishing a Packard, just as in *Chinatown*.[18]

Because the artificial style in which the story is presented identifies it as a fiction, its status as a creation of the human imagination can become its subject. The film proposes an ironic reinterpretation of the private-eye genre in which the conventional pattern of heroic self-determination played out by Gittes is contradicted by a self-conscious critique of the formula carried by the film's images, a critique that sees the hero's control over his world as an illusion. This critique overpowers the traditional generic structure at the story's conclusion, instating another, more disturbing order, which the conventional form had previously hidden.

As Garrett Stewart has pointed out, some of the devices of dramatic foreboding purposely subvert the narrative's formulaic expectations.[19] In anticipation of the final catastrophe, for example, attention is repeatedly drawn to Evelyn Mulwray's eyes, and her slump against the horn on her car is presaged by a similar "accident" when she is explaining to Gittes why she is hiding her "sister" Katherine. Such references invest the unconventional conclusion with an eerie feeling of inevitability that has nothing to do with the film's ostensible plot.

Polanski's recurring deep-focus three-shots similarly undercut generic expectations by defining shifting power relationships in which Gittes is not always visually as privileged as his cocky, tough-guy attitude assumes. Though Huston had employed a similar strategy of three-shots in *The Maltese Falcon*, Bogart almost always dominated the other characters in the frame by virture of his superior height or positioning. Nicholson, however, is not so favored by Polanski. Gittes's scenes with police officers Escobar and Loach and with civic officials Yelburton and Mulvihill typically find the hero either boxed in or pushed to the side of the frame: visual expressions of his ultimate helplessness in the face of greater numbers. Evelyn Mulwray is also portrayed in this way. When Escobar interviews her in the morgue, he stands to her right. To escape his disturbing questions, she tries to turn away, only to be startled by Loach, who is lurking on the left side of the broad Panavision composition. A variation of this episode climaxes the film when Gittes puts out his left arm to divert Escobar's gunfire from Evelyn's car, only to find that by so doing he has activated others, including the more callous Loach on his right, whose gun is raised the moment Escobar's is lowered, a final hydralike image of malignant bureaucratic proliferation.

The film's use of deep space works not only to prefigure the fate of Evelyn and Gittes but also in a different way to designate Cross as the malignant force that lies behind the mystery. When Gittes first goes to visit the old man, Cross approaches the detective's car in an atypically centered shot taken from Gittes's point of view through the windshield of the automobile. Cross takes a position in the middle of the frame, flanked by his lackeys. His figure is powerfully underscored by the symmetrical art-deco pattern on the car's dashboard, which appears at the bottom of the picture. A similar motif is repeated in Gittes's final showdown scene with Cross. There we see the old man coming into Evelyn's house from Gittes's position on the patio. Walking into the entry hall toward the detective, he is carefully centered on the patio door frame and further centered by the frame of the front door behind him. The strong formal symmetry in both of these scenes designates Cross as a person of entrenched power, the man at the center of things, and also as a figure toward whom all paths will inevitably lead—despite the seemingly serendipitous meanderings of the mystery-adventure plot.

The Hero as Spectator

The implications of Polanski's self-conscious view of fantasy are most fully expressed in the way he depicts his hero. As a hard-boiled detective, Jack Nicholson's J. J. Gittes embodies the values such heroes represent. He aspires to actions on a grand scale, ostensibly motivated by ideals of courage, justice, and altruism, in contrast to Escobar, Duffy, and Walsh. By self-consciously playing against the hard-boiled formula's realist pretensions, however, Polanski, at a deeper level, calls these values into question. In *Chinatown* the private-eye myth is revealed as "inadequate and destructive" because of the bigotry nurtured by its theme of tough-guy individualism. The hard-boiled detective story typically designates minorities (often Orientals) and women as sources of corruption. The hero's task was to find them out and confront them. *The Maltese Falcon* is again paradigmatic: the villains are closely associated with the Orient, which is portrayed as a place where amorality and greed run rampant; and the most villainous character of all is a woman: sexual, duplicitous, and deadly. Because the hero refuses to be tempted by the exotic splendor of the former or the sensual pleasures of the latter, he emerges triumphant.[20]

Gittes has wholeheartedly accepted this view of the world, believing that the way out of Chinatown is the way to success and happiness. He measures his superiority in part by his ability to ridicule Orientals and women, speaking disparagingly about them and making clumsy jokes at their expense. (He also makes a gratuitous joke about Jews at the Mar Vista rest home.) A man who patronizes his girlish receptionist, Gittes cheerfully agrees with his first client's pronouncement on the female sex: "They're all whores." His style is set against that of Hollis Mulwray, who has Oriental servants, a Spanish-speaking "girlfriend," and a wife. Gittes believes his salvation lies in avoiding such associations; Mulwray embraces them. The water commissioner's integrity also separates him from the rest of society, for Escobar, Loach, Duffy, Walsh, and the proprietor of the Mar Vista Rest Home all give evidence that they see the world in the same divided way Gittes does.

The film, however, does not. In contrast to earlier versions of the formula, in which the narrative was constructed to validate the hero's values, *Chinatown* concludes by revealing them as paranoid projections cloaking the protagonist's own sense of impotence in the face of the byzantine complexity and evil of modern life. Director John Huston here portrays a man whose power allows him to impose his most extreme and perverse fantasies on the world. Noah Cross can act out his desires with almost unlimited freedom and virtually no moral constraints. In a sense, Huston is playing himself; for a film director, too, enjoys the power to impose his fantasies on others, on viewers who may accept them as simply "the way things are"—just as the characters in *Chinatown* accept the situation Noah Cross creates as "reality." Lest we miss the point, Polanski has cast himself as a lesser denizen of Huston's virulent kingdom. But his own private-eye fantasy, though it may be equally perverse, is less naive. Here, as in other Polanski films, the impulse to re-create the world in art becomes a sinister enterprise in which artistic form becomes a means of disguising and vicariously fulfilling wishes of an unspeakable nature.

Needing to assert his own sense of power and control over a threatening world, Gittes repeatedly constructs theories from inadequate or ill-digested information; and these theories are invariably at odds with the actual situation, making him ultimately responsible for the disaster that concludes the action. His vulnerability and moral deformity appear metaphorically in his slashed nose, and the universality of his weakness is suggested by the disease and physical disabilities that mark others among the film's characters: both Escobar and the abnormally overweight mortician have colds, the boy at the Hall of Records sports a large boil, and one of the youths in the orange grove is on crutches.

The shortcomings of Gittes's theories arise most often from his tendency to see Mulwray's widow, Evelyn, as the perpetrator of the crimes, a tendency that becomes conspicuous from the time he makes love to her. Evelyn's image connotes not only sexual but also racial otherness, for her features are made up to give them a decidedly Oriental cast, with geisha-like bows painted on her lips under thin, rounded eyebrows. In many of her scenes full frontal lighting flattens her features into an even more strikingly Oriental configuration.

Lying beside Evelyn after they have gone to bed together, Gittes is quick to disregard her request to wait for her at her house while she goes to visit the girl Katherine. Later, outside Katherine's hideout, the detective dismisses Evelyn's attempt to explain the situation, and then dismisses her as well, choosing not to go home with her and not even to see her again until the climactic scene in which he confronts her as her husband's murderer.

Unable to trust Evelyn enough to achieve a stable sexual relationship, the detective ultimately resorts to slapping her. The episode in which he does so recalls an analogous scene in *The Maltese Falcon*, where Humphrey Bogart's physical abuse of Mary Astor is smoothly rationalized by providing the hero with a clear justification for his behavior. Unlike Gittes, Bogart's explanation of events does not reflect his own inadequacies; instead it is presented as an accurate re-creation of the actual state of affairs. Bogart is always right, and he always acts for the best. The hard-boiled formula is constructed to excuse the hero's behavior by means of such rationalizations. Polanski's version of the story, however, allows no such refuge in thematic assertions of verisimilitude or morality. What we see in *Chinatown* is a depiction of a man abusing a woman, an act that the private-eye genre has in the past construed as heroic rather than perverse. After his misguided release of energy, Gittes is confronted by Evelyn's daughter standing on the stairs. Faced with this symbol of his own limited vision, he can only look confused and defeated: trapped in his destructive rationalizations and unable to comprehend the insecurities that lie beneath them, he cannot imagine how he could have contributed to a happier outcome.

Later he further acts out the rituals of power and self-assertion propagated by the private-eye fantasy by contriving a fruitless showdown with the real villain, Noah Cross. Meanwhile, Evelyn's chances of escape and freedom dwindle to nothing. "I was trying to stop someone from being hurt," Gittes recalls of his earlier experiences with a woman. "I ended up making sure that she was hurt." *Chinatown* explores the culturally conditioned displacement of guilt onto the weak, which inevitably leads to such transformations from desire into destruction.

Gittes's guilt is represented by the image of Chinatown, the place in which he was once advised to do "as little as possible." It is characterized as a world in which the individual is helpless in the face of the complex intrigues surrounding him and where depravity exists on a scale that defies the imagination. At first, the hero believes that he has escaped from this world; however, the film's pervasive Chinese motif, increasingly associated with Gittes's growing relationship with Evelyn Mulwray, forecasts the detective's return to it. Though Gittes is warned of imminent danger by Cross, who tells him early on that "you may think you know what you're dealing with, but believe me, you don't," he persists in his fateful course. The physical place he finally arrives at in the film's concluding scene—a dark, desolate, and tawdry street in the "other" part of town—gives visual expression to his demoralized and debilitated spiritual state.

The catalyst of this transformation is spectatorship. Polanski often frames Gittes in profile at the side of the image as he observes the cinematic world. Spying is, after all, his business. He makes his living by exposing others, observing them from a position that, he assumes, carries with it invisibility, invulnerability, and an unquestionable professional detachment. When Evelyn Mulwray asks him why he wants to know her maiden name, he responds, "No reason; I'm just a snoop." And when the Mulwray case begins to threaten his own reputation, he insists, "I'm not the one who's supposed to be caught with his pants down." Later, Gittes acts on his conviction that he must remain invulnerable by getting up and almost walking away when Noah Cross inquires about his relationship with Evelyn.

As the formula has it, he is right: his own motives should be beyond question. But in *Chinatown* the detective not only observes—and judges—others, but also is observed—and judged—himself. As Evelyn points out early in the film, "No question from you is innocent." Gittes's inability to remain innocent first appears as he begins watching Mulwray. Though he favors a vantage point above his prey, it quickly becomes apparent that even this superior stance cannot guarantee his impregnability. At the ocean, he must jump back to avoid Mulwray's return glance. And later the detective is forced to retreat in a similar fashion when he accidentally loosens some gravel from the roof of the El Macondo apartments, where Mulwray is visiting Katherine.

In Polanski's private-eye story, the hero's position as spectator is not always a privileged one. From time to time, other points of view intrude ominously. Near the opening of the film, the camera moves out of Gittes's range as he watches Hollis Mulwray at the ocean, closing in on the face of a stranger whose concerns remain cloaked and puzzling. Later, during Gittes's lunch with Noah Cross, the old man is shot head-on as he stands and turns away from the detective to tell him that he and Mulwray were arguing about "my daughter." Moments like these reverberate with hidden meanings to which the hero is not privy. Gittes, however, ignores these indications of his own limitations. As a result, he invites the gaze of Evelyn Mulwray at a moment when his adolescent bigotry is most apparent. As he is recounting the off-color "Chinaman" joke to Duffy and Walsh, the camera shows us what Gittes cannot see: Evelyn Mulwray standing silently behind him observing his performance.

The judgment implied by Evelyn's disdainful gaze seems just, for the sleuthing activities about which Gittes takes such smug pride seem slightly contemptible. Unlike the Bogart hero, whose image of integrity allowed him to watch and judge with impunity, Gittes seems a professional voyeur of a disreputable and disturbing sort. During the opening scene we find that he has intruded on the sexual privacy of a client's wife, and yet his attitude toward such a gross violation of decency is callously unthinking: it is his job. He approaches the Mulwray case with the same carelessly assured detachment, but in this case his spying makes him not only blameworthy but also vulnerable.

In a sense, Gittes's perpetual looking has always involved him in consequences, though his determination to do "as little as possible" has limited the weight of the responsibility he has assumed. As the film progresses, he is confronted with ever more graphic displays of violence and devastation. His spying on Curly's wife leads to her eye being blackened; his spying on Hollis Mulwray's widow, however, leads to her eye being blasted from its socket. In the first instance, the issues are of limited importance and the result comic: in the second, the issues are monumental and the result disastrous. Yet he remains trapped in the private-eye fantasy of his own invincible heroism and eventual triumph.

His commitment to vicarious pleasure and to the illusion of passive invulnerability is shared by the audience, which has come to enjoy the film's fantasy. Polanski equates himself as a creator of such fantasies with both the protagonist and the spectators early in the action by the use of lenses or frames that suggest the filmic apparatus. Gittes scrutinizes the dried Los Angeles riverbed through binoculars, a view re-created on the screen by a double iris shot. His observations of Mulwray are framed by the windshield of his car on one occasion, by his rear-view mirror on another.

Chinatown is permeated with photographs—frozen records of ongoing human interaction—and they are charged with implications of veiled sexual desire and evaded moral responsibility. It opens with a photograph of sexual intercourse and ends with a lifelike evocation of violence and cruelty. In the meantime, we, along with the hero, are invited to look at increasingly graphic depictions of erotic encounters and brutal assaults. "You know she murdered Mulwray," Escobar accuses Gittes. "You were there, you took pictures of it." And if Gittes had been there, is that what he would have done? Like Gittes, we in the audience may watch because we wish to judge without being judged ourselves. But *Chinatown* unmasks our desire and the sadistic sexual impulses underlying it.

Gittes is himself a member of an audience near the opening of the film when the Alta Vallejo dam is discussed. Mayor Bagby, the dam's sponsor, is shot from below against a blown-up photograph of Roosevelt. The shot recalls Charles Foster Kane during his election speech in *Citizen Kane*, one of Polanski's favorite films. In Welles's story, an observer in the audience, Jim Gettys (from whom Polanski's hero probably derives his own name), becomes a participant by putting Kane's picture in the paper and thereby making public the scandal of Kane's private life—a role Gittes himself inadvertently takes on, much to his own shock and dismay.

In *Citizen Kane* Welles uses cinema to bring the private life of a man into the public domain, and Polanski examines a similar theme in his own film. *Chinatown* recalls *Citizen Kane* not only by the Jim Gettys motif but also by the "No Trespassing" signs, which are prominent at the beginning of Welles's film and throughout Polanski's. The first time Gittes ignores such a sign he gets his nose slashed by the director. The second time, he is brutally beaten by a family of farmers. Eventually, Gittes cracks Claude Mulvihill's skull against the camera lens, directly assaulting not only Mulvihill but also the voyeuristic pleasure the audience is capable of taking in cinematic fantasy.

And yet, even when the detective confronts Evelyn, we continue to believe in our own safety, remaining convinced that the private-eye formula will operate to justify the tough-guy hero's code. But this time it does not. The denouement shows us yet another audience, an audience of Chinese, gawking at the spectacle of Evelyn Mulwray's blood-smeared body. These Orientals are not mysterious and threatening perpetrators of crime. They are spectators. Like most spectators, they are silent, power-

less, sensation-seeking. The object of their gaze is the same as that of
Gittes's, and of our own: the desecrated body of a woman. *Chinatown*
concludes with an extraordinary crane shot that connects all of the film's
major characters as well as the Oriental voyeurs in a single continuous
motion containing only one unobtrusive cut, then pulls up and back to
take in the entire scene—a scene in which the narrative resolution is revealed as the expression of the dark side of our own fantasy lives.

The Mythology of History

Chinatown's examination of realism encompasses not only the conventions of the hard-boiled detective genre but also the constructions of social
and physical reality, which are part of the realist aesthetic. Here again,
what audiences ordinarily accept as reality is exposed as myth, for the
"myth" of progress has also traditionally been portrayed in realistic terms.

Chinatown suggests that, like its private-eye hero, who seems fated to
return again and again to the morally degenerate atmosphere of Chinatown, history itself repeats cycles of reform and disillusionment. Though
some commentators have criticized the film's critique of American capital-
ism as limited,[21] it actually offers a broad perspective on the nature of historical process. Here, as in many of Polanski's other films, this process is
suggested by images of water.

Chinatown achieves its impact, however, not by abstracting its images
of water, as happens in Polanski's more modernist films, but by connecting
them to particular political phenomena. As many of the initial reviews noted, the story's portrayal of scandal and corruption in the highest places
during the 1930s bears striking similarities to the post-Watergate climate
that prevailed in the United States when the film was initially released.
Robert Towne's issue-oriented script is based on the Owens River Valley
scandal, the paradigmatic controversy over water rights in a state that is
still in the process of "inventing itself with water."[22] Though the scandal
occurred at the turn of the century, water rights remain the key to California's growth and prosperity, and the violent conflicts depicted in the film
were reenacted during the early 1970s when yet another aqueduct was
proposed to bring water to Owens Valley.

The film's version of the story follows populist accounts that see the Los
Angeles drought as an artificially created ploy to persuade the people of
the city to support a water project designed to benefit a few large land-
holders. At the center of the controversy was Water Commissioner William Mullholland, a visionary who has been credited with having more to
do with the creation of the modern city of Los Angeles than any other
single individual.[23] As the prototype for *Chinatown*'s Hollis Mulwray,
Mulholland harbored a deep love for Los Angeles. "It was the most attractive town I had ever seen," he wrote in an autobiographical sketch. "The

people were hospitable. There was plenty to do and a fair compensation offered for whatever you did. . . . The Los Angeles river was the greatest attraction. It was a beautiful, limpid little stream with willows on its banks. . . . It was so attractive to me that it at once became something about which my whole schema of life was woven."[24]

Towne set the action of *Chinatown* in 1937, later than the Owens River Valley scandal, but appreciably earlier than classic cinematic examples of the hard-boiled genre such as *The Maltese Falcon* and *The Big Sleep*, both of which were set in the 1940s. The late 1930s, however, was a time of noteworthy public-works programs, specifically programs connected with Roosevelt's New Deal policies. In 1937 these programs were temporarily cut back, and the brief recession that followed gave rise to a renewed commitment to extensive public-works projects as a means of revitalizing the economy. The 1937 experience gave rise to the theory that the government, through a policy of liberal spending, could help pull the nation out of a depression.

Chinatown plays on these historical associations, offering a disdainfully revisionist view of the way in which the New Deal economic policies actually operated. A photograph of Roosevelt hanging behind Gittes's desk is prominent in the film's opening scene. At the civic hearing, a similar portrait hangs behind Mayor Bagby. The dam is enthusiastically hailed by the audience at the hearing, an audience composed of members of the farming community from which Roosevelt drew a major part of his support. Later, however, it becomes clear that the project has not been designed to benefit these people at all but rather to provide even greater wealth for a handful of landowners who have engineered an elaborate scheme to defraud the city and its taxpayers. When Gittes wonders what else these latter-day robber barons could possibly wish to own that could justify such machinations, Noah Cross, who has masterminded the scheme, replies, "The future!", a chilling statement of the limitlessness of capitalist greed.

Gittes, who wishes to take on Mulwray's progressive vision following the latter's death, undergoes a kind of baptism when a sudden torrent of water gushes through a culvert, engulfing him; and he emerges from the reservoir enclosure without a shoe. The lack of a shoe is a conspicuous feature of Mulwray's corpse as we see it being hauled up a similar culvert. Gittes, however, is finally unable to step into Mulwray's shoes in any morally meaningful way, for Mulwray, unlike Gittes, is someone who, in his own words, "won't make the same mistake twice."

The ideal of progress advanced in the conventional histories of our culture is thus rejected as what Hayden White has characterized as a "specifically Western prejudice by which the presumed superiority of modern industrial society can be retroactively substantiated."[25] The "progress" represented by legendary figures like Mulholland and Roosevelt is seen here as mere myth, a fiction created by powerful capitalists like Noah Cross to rationalize their own will to domination. By alluding to historiographic codes of other cultures, *Chinatown* suggests that the cyclic pattern it unearths in modern America is a universal one. These allusions also involve water.

Cross's role as the force that prevents reform is suggested by a series of allusions that echo the Grail legend. Moreover, the name Noah Cross recalls the Old Testament patriarch who also profited from a natural disaster involving the earth's water supply. A further series of references recalls the story of Oedipus, which similarly features a "detective" who seeks to save a blighted city by solving a murder only to discover an incestuous secret, the revelation of which leads to further disaster and the destruction of the eyes of one of the story's major characters.[26] All of these allusions, illustrate the ways in which history is created to mask and reformulate the repeated betrayal of the promise of progress. In the historical myths of other cultures, we readily recognize this function; in our own, however, we have granted history a privileged reality through the imprimatur of science.

Myths of Natural Order

The realism offered by science, too, the film rejects as myth. Though *Chinatown*'s mise-en-scène offers a "realistic" portrayal of nature, the film questions our conventional perceptions of it. Polanski's visual style emphasizes the long takes and deep focus long associated with cinematic realism, yet the impression of redeemed physical reality is undermined by repeated images of the fundamental unintelligibility of the natural world.[27] After revealing the corpse of the false Mrs. Mulwray, for instance, the camera focuses on a spilled bag of groceries. And when Gittes confronts a young Mexican boy in the Los Angeles riverbed, the barren landscape, eerily luminous light, and atonal music invest the scene with a feeling of uncanny strangeness.

Such a depiction of the physical environment challenges the comfortable, "domesticated" quality nature has acquired in our culture through the process of rational ordering developed by science. In *Chinatown* this ordering process is portrayed as still another fiction of historical progress. As Michel Foucault has pointed out, since the nineteenth century "history has become the unavoidable element in our thought." In the realm of natural science, this historicizing tendency manifested itself in an *organic* view of nature, which, according to Foucault, "was to deploy in a temporal series, the analogies that connect distinct organic structures to one another."[28] These presuppositions form the foundations of modern biology, and have become the axioms by which people today construct a natural order based on the notion of a gradual progression over time to more complex forms of life. Such an "evolutionary" perspective serves to rationalize humankind's domination over "lower forms" of life. The radical skepticism Polanski acquired from his modernist background leads him to attack this "progressive" vision of nature as he attacks the progressive visions generated by social histories and by popular generic forms. In this area also, his critique is carried by the film's images of water.

In *Chinatown* the modern progressive vision of science is again represented by the figure of Hollis Mulwray, a man who "loved tidepools because that was where life begins," but who eventually meets his death in just such a tidepool. Mulwray, who in Cross's words "made this city," lives in a house set on the only verdant land we see in the film, and portraits of similarly verdant scenery decorate his office walls. As the personification of a progressive vision of nature as well as of history. Mulwray acts as the guardian of the public water supply.

By contrast, Cross is repeatedly associated with images of fish, which suggest a regression of life rather than an evolution of it. This primitive imagery suggests a nature governed by chaos, a vision of natural disorder that permeates the entire film. For *Chinatown* evokes the terrifying possibility that the orderly separation between water and land could break down, thereby destroying all higher forms of life—including humankind. While Los Angeles is in the middle of a serious drought, two people are drowned, and Gittes himself, in two frightening scenes, is almost overcome by sudden and unexpected bursts of water that are accompanied by ominous rumblings. As Mayor Bagby, speaking for the Alto Vallejo dam project, warns, "We live on the edge of an ocean, but we also live on the edge of a desert. Los Angeles is a desert community. Beneath our streets lies a desert. And without water, the dust will rise up and cover us as though we had never existed."

All of the allusions to water cited in *Chinatown* ultimately represent the attempts made by various cultures to allay anxieties about a primitive force that must be controlled and regulated before civilization—and, indeed, life itself—can exist. In one sense, then, the detective's mission is to find the secret of the waters and by so doing to revitalize the myth of a progressive natural and social order. But Gittes can neither effect reform in Los Angeles nor achieve personal fulfillment. The reassurances offered by all traditional theories of progress are thus similar to the reassurances offered by traditional generic forms; all such theories are simply forms of generic codes.

By embracing the codes of traditional realism, *Chinatown* speaks to its audience not only as individuals but also as members of a culture for which the myths embodied by particular generic, historical, and scientific representations play an important role. It is thus the best example of the way in which the social and political exigencies of the film industry have forced Polanski to speak to a larger public, encouraging him to communicate on a cultural as well as a personal level. Rather than simply echoing the cultural myths that rationalize various modes of domination, however, Polanski's aggressive modernism has modeled a film that asks us to question our own participation in such processes. By upsetting the genre, *Chinatown* exposes the self-justifying structures through which the popular myths of our culture naturalize ideology.

6

Sexuality Redeemed: *Tess*

IT IS HARD TO IMAGINE a more perfect comeback film than *Tess* for a man whose directorial career had been seriously endangered by the sensational events of his personal life. After having escaped from the United States in order to avoid serving the prison term he had been sentenced to for sexual misconduct with a minor, Polanski settled in France. There, on a budget of over $6 million, he produced an impeccable and elegant adaptation of a major literary classic, shot in Brittany, Normandy, and the Paris region on a thirty-week schedule. After receiving three French Academy Awards, *Tess* was released in the United States to critical and popular acclaim, winning Oscars for Geoffrey Unsworth and Ghislain Clouquet (cinematography), Anthony Powell (costume design), and Jack Stephens (art direction). The film's dedication, "To Sharon," reminded audiences of the well-publicized tragedy of which the director himself was a victim. The narrative emphasizes the explicitly feminist cast of Thomas Hardy's novel about a peasant girl whose life is ruined when she is sexually compromised by a man above her station. This sympathetic treatment of female victimization inspired some reviewers to term it an "atonement." Moreover, Polanski's decision to star the seventeen-year-old Nastassia Kinski, with whom he himself had been romantically involved, presented him as someone who could act as a mentor to young girls rather than as one who merely exploited them.

Tess marks an important change for Polanski. It is at once his most classical film and his most personal one. Speaking of *Tess*, Polanski has said, "I think that today it is somehow more proper to reach out to the literature of the nineteenth century or the first half of the twentieth, literature that deals more with sentiments and feelings than with style."[1] The explicit sex and violence that characterized the director's earlier work are absent here. "When I was making my first films, I did scenes of violence and sex because the general hypocrisy didn't allow that," Polanski told an interviewer. "Now violence has been exploited to such an extent that I am tired of it and nostalgic for romance."[2] His decision to turn away from coldly stylized shock effects was not a sudden one. "Kenneth Tynan, who loved *Re-*

109

pulsion, wrote that he was waiting for something more from me, something that said something profound about life . . . perhaps something not as cold as my past work, something warmer," the director commented in 1969. "I thought it was a very important point and I thought about it a great deal."[3]

The break between *Tess* and Polanski's prior films can be explained in terms of a new, more accepting attitude he has taken toward his audience. *Tess* does not subject us to heavy doses of subliminal emotional attack by playing on the most perverse aspects of our pleasure in pictures and stories. Instead the film opens with an effortless visual and aural transition from asynchronic to synchronic modalities. As the credits fade up on the phrase "based on a novel by Thomas Hardy," they shift from stark flashes of white on a black ground to a softer format of scroll-like unrolling over a rural countryside, disappearing unobtrusively into the pastel gray sky. A little later, the music dissolves from Phillippe Sarde's lyrical symphonic overture to the folk melody played by the amateur musicians accompanying the May Day dancers. We are thus placed in an unhostile world in which the narrative presence of the filmmaker is in harmony with his material, not in conflict with it.

This new sense of harmony is best understood by examining the ways in which the film has emphasized and modified certain aspects of the novel. Hardy's struggle with the social and intellectual upheavals of the Victorian age in *Tess of the D'Urbervilles* challenged and expanded Polanski's own vision, leading him to examine the roots of his own nihilism. Though many reviewers found *Tess* a lifeless translation of the book, the director has altered his source material in order to incorporate his characteristic themes and motifs in muted form. *Tess* is his most "realistic" film, portraying the unforced harmonies of a naturalized world in which fantasy and grotesquerie are largely absent.[4]

Writing about the present, Hardy could only wonder where the conflicts he portrayed could lead. In an often-quoted line from the novel, the heroine conveys this uncertainty. "[You] seem to see numbers of tomorrows just all in a line," Tess says, "the first of them the biggest and clearest, the others getting smaller and smaller as they stand farther away; but they all seem very fierce and cruel and as if they said, 'I'm coming! Beware of me! Beware of me!' "[5] Polanski, in fact, has experienced the fierce and cruel future that Hardy guessed at. Despairing about our own age, Polanski finds hope in the past. *Tess* is a nostalgic film, a look at a time when life seemed to offer possibilities that have since vanished. Polanski portrays the nineteenth century as the end of an era when people could achieve the sense of integrity and purpose that grows out of an easy coexistence with a natural and social order. If Hardy's *Tess of the D'Urbervilles* can be seen as a tract calling for a change in social conditions, Polanski's film evokes a time when change was about to end the possibility of a coherent sense of personal authenticity. This nostalgic vision has led the director to a new, more optimistic solution to an issue that has plagued him through his career, the issue of sexual domination.

In *Tess*, for the first time, Polanski portrays mature sexual fulfillment. His ability to do so is the result of a more sympathetic understanding of women than he has shown in the past. In his modernist films, the director's interest in abstracted and stylized games of power led him to present caricatured portraits of women as victims or viragoes. In his commercial projects, however, he was prompted to examine interrelationships between cultural patterns and individual psychology through more extended linear narratives and developed, humanized characterizations. Thus Carol Ledoux in *Repulsion*, Rosemary Woodhouse in *Rosemary's Baby*, and Evelyn Mulwray in *Chinatown* are all victimized by complicated social and psychological forces. Their violent impulses are reactions to these forces. Having portrayed and understood the mechanisms of sexual oppression in these early films, Polanski was able, in *Tess*, to envision the emotional transcendence of that oppression. Though Tess's fulfillment is depicted in the film as a private and fleeting one, achieved through a moment of sexual rapture, it is the only such moment of mature erotic bliss in all of Polanski's oeuvre.

Nature and Art

Industrialism, which took human beings from the soil, uprooted them from tradition. The end of the agrarian system signaled the end of a sense of an accommodating interchange between people and their surroundings. Though Hardy and Polanski view it in different contexts, this change represents an important theme for both of them. Polanski emphasizes the novel's motif of journeys, including even more such scenes than are in the book. Angel Clare, the man Tess marries, rushes on ahead to the wedding as his bride-to-be tries desperately to unburden herself to him. Alec D'Urberville, the man responsible for her shame, dogs Tess's tracks as she accompanies her family to their new quarters at Kingsbere after the death of her father. Tess catches Angel on the train as it is about to pull away from Sandbourne, the seaside village where she has just murdered Alec. These scenes and others (many of which, as in the novel, take place in fast-moving vehicles) show the world moving at a dizzying pace. They point to the coming inability of human beings to adapt to the relentless speed of the machine age.

The eternal cycles of nature, however, are more hospitable. It is true that in *Tess*, as in most of Polanski's other films, there are repulsive images of the aged and infirm, unsavory reminders of death and human frailty: Alec D'Urberville's mother, with her sightless, staring gaze; the palsied minister who presides over Tess and Angel's wedding; the vacant-faced idiot son of the housekeeper at Wellbridge, where Tess and Angel spend their abortive honeymoon. But in this film we also find portraits of benign and engaging old people like the onlookers at the May Day dance and Dairyman Crick, Tess's employer during her romance with Angel at Talbothays dairy. These images suggest an acceptance of aging and death that appears nowhere else in Polanski's oeuvre; they create a vision of the human life cycle as an integral part of nature.

Polanski has said that "nature plays an important role in the film, a mysterious, hidden side of nature which resists startling, overdramatic effects."[6] Both novel and film betray a nostalgic longing for an organic unity between humanity and nature. Hardy celebrates nature through lengthy descriptions in which human actions are enhanced by natural processes. Polanski takes full advantage of the Panavision frame to exploit the novel's inclination toward scenic contemplation. The picturesque depictions of Tess wandering outside of her parents' house before her visit to Alec D'Urberville at Trantridge and after her return testify to her alliance with the landscape, which echoes her apprehension and sorrow. Her revitalizing romance with Angel is played out among the "flowers, leaves, nightingales, thrushes, and such ephemeral creatures" at Talbothays (109); her penance following his rejection amid "the morning frosts and afternoon rains" of Flintcomb-Ash where she is later employed in the turnip fields (239).

If nature is beautiful, however, it is also cruel. Polanski's portrait of the forbidding gray mud at Flintcomb-Ash and the scene of Tess's family huddling together in a makeshift tent at Kingsbere (both reproduced from the book) make nature's harshness palpable. At the end of the opening scene, an ominous wind comes up, and it returns later, accompanied by a violent thunderstorm.

Though natural phenomena are subtly integrated into the narrative, Polanski includes a few touches that look forward to a modern sense of what Hardy calls the "serene dissociation" of the universe (25). Hedge clippers snap ominously, buzzing flies add a vaguely dissonant note as Tess tastes Alec's strawberries and again as the camera tracks slowly around the milkmaids' room at Talbothays dairy. This later scene ends with a shot of udderlike sacs that drip with the whey used for cheesemaking. Such details endow nature with the alien, slightly sinister aspect it exudes in films like *Knife in the Water* and *Cul-de-Sac*. As the action progresses, there are more chilling images, taken from Hardy, of the machines which, in our time, have overwhelmed the natural world, and which are indifferent to human beings.

The image of the machine suggests a newly disturbing kind of human awareness. Hardy's novel has been seen as an expression of the conflicts of modern self-consciousness.[7] This dilemma is communicated by the novel's major characters. Hardy depicts them in terms of their inner divisions and turmoil, thereby reflecting "the fascination with evolving consciousness" which helped define the beginnings of modernism.[8] Angel, most obviously, is affected by the conflicting intellectual currents of the day. The tortured clash of passion and intellect that wracks him after hearing Tess's confession is presented from an internalized perspective. Similarly, Alec's conversion to religion and subsequent backsliding provide multiple opportunities for speculative conversations between himself and Tess on the role of religion in people's lives.

The film's characters, though intellectually simplified, are even more ambiguous. For Polanski, human identity is ultimately enigmatic, giving rise to a vision of character as mask. Tess often appears, like Carol in *Repulsion*, merely as a blank slate, reacting to the events around her as a mirror, expressionless and opaque. And the modes of masking can become more complex and problematic. Peter Firth's portrayal of Angel plays the sweet naïveté of his appearance against the emotional atrocity he will commit against Tess. In the film's opening scene, Tess's father, Jack Durbyfield, unexpectedly discovers that he is descended from a noble family. The camera lingers on a close shot that mercilessly magnifies his weak, grizzled chin, shifty, bloodshot eyes, and decaying teeth. The contrast between his designated nobility and his degenerate appearance creates ambiguities about the definition of self perhaps deeper than those conveyed in Hardy's prose.

Because such ambiguities are bottomless, the intellectual struggle to know the self becomes ultimately absurd. Angel, the most "modern" character, indulges in some absurdist humor following his short-sighted rejection of his new bride. "Have mercy," he muses, then repeats the phrase. In the novel, this line is given to Tess, and there is no suggestion of the kind of double entendre implied by the reference to Mercy Chant, Angel's other marital prospect (192). The director comments on his character's callously shallow linguistic play a little later, when his camera catches the slogan "Blessed are the merciful" painted on a rail fence. By such dislocations, the pretensions of language to make meaningful connections between the human consciousness and the real world are called into question.

Beneath such pretensions lies a deeper malignancy. Like many of Polanski's other films, *Tess* portrays self-consciousness as a perverse psychological process. Self-awareness is expressed as an awareness of being watched—an element present in the novel but exploited more fully in the film. In contrast to Polanski's earlier films, however, self-consciousness in *Tess* is incipient and tentative: the looks in this film are typically benign and relatively naive. Children peer out of doorways in the background of scenes; and the wondering reactions of Tess's saucer-eyed youngest sister are frequently recorded. Animals watch: a deer observes Tess sleeping in the woods; a horse, pulling a milk cart, gazes blankly ahead as Tess falters in her first attempt to confess her sins to Angel.

Other instances of watching in which humiliation and guilt are exposed begin to suggest a darker side of self-consciousness. In Rolliver's tavern the old men of Marlott, the town in which Tess's family lives, gaze at Jack Durbyfield as he makes a spectacle of his newfound pretension to nobility. At Wellbridge, the imbecilic son of the housekeeper stares emptily at Angel as he impatiently explains why his wife has left him. The caretaker of Bramshurst Court, the vacant house in which Tess and Angel rest briefly during their flight from the police, surprises the fugitives in bed together. And the landlady at Sandbourne peers through the keyhole at Tess and Alec quarreling just before the murder (this last point of view reproduced from the novel). Such observers, who may be more judging, suggest a projected and externalized conscience. In Polanski's earlier psychological studies such as *Repulsion* and *The Tenant*, which have contemporary settings, this splitting of consciousness goes to much further extremes, leading to alienation, paranoia, and ultimately to the total disintegration of integrity. In *Tess*, however, this process is just beginning, and as yet the characters are largely able to maintain a beguiling innocence.

Their innocence is based on their capacity for emotional spontaneity. Polanski sympathetically emphasizes moments of emotional crises in his characters' lives. When Tess discovers her letter to Angel under the rug, for instance, the image fades to white for a few seconds; and when Angel hears Tess's confessions after their marriage and later at Sandbourne, his emotional upheaval is indicated by rack focus shots, which shift from Tess's face during her difficult unburdenings, to Angel's as he grasps the implications of what she is saying. The intensity of such moments is enhanced by dramatic intrusion of the passionate musical score.

"I'm happy," Alec confesses as he rides through the forest with Tess. "I want to prolong the moment." It is a vain wish, for happiness is too fragile to be easily prolonged. In *Tess* there are continual breaks in the emotional rhythm, some reproduced from the novel, others added. Tess and Angel's first kiss in the farmyard is interrupted by the lowing of a cow. Another embrace is punctuated by the snores of a farmhand asleep in a pile of hay. Tess's flight of fancy at the breakfast table at Talbothays is both begun and ended by loud burps from Marian, another milkmaid. Less happy moments are, by contrast, painfully prolonged. Angel and Tess's breakfast at Wellbridge following their wedding is eaten in silence; we hear only the ticking of a clock.

Polanski's vision is thus grounded in evanescent emotional truths rather than enduring systematic ones. Religion is, therefore, given little credence in the film. As in the novel, church practices are mocked in the figures of the hypocritical vicar of Marlott and the prudish Reverend

Clare. Like Hardy, Polanski attributes Angel's rejection of Tess in part to the repressive religious morality he has learned from his straightlaced country-parson family. And later, when the two are at Stonehenge, Tess asks, as in the novel, "Did they sacrifice to God here?"—reminding us that scapegoating has always been part of religious ritual.

But in the film no distinction is made between the church and Christianity itself, a distinction implied in the novel by the penchant of Hardy's narrator for scriptural aphorisms.[9] In contrast, Tess's attempt to baptize her own baby is not directly shown in the film. Polanski suppresses the spiritual issues to concentrate on maximizing the personal and social ones. As Tess recounts the makeshift baptismal ceremony she has performed, the camera focuses on the reaction of the vicar: his embarrassment, timidity, and self-protectiveness easily outweigh his capacity for fairness and compassion. He has been interrupted while beekeeping: a mildly dangerous occupation for which he wears a protective costume—a variation on the clerical garb, which grants him social immunity from any barbs of anger his inhumanity might arouse in ill-treated parishioners such as the one who now stands before him. The bees buzzing in the background during his interview with Tess echo our sense of his irritation at her intrusion. Tess, by contrast, remains more vulnerable. In her brown crocheted shawl, she looks birdlike. A similar association is suggested at other points in the film as well to invoke both her "naturalness" and her helplessness. But, when the vicar refuses to grant her baby a Christian burial, she nonetheless responds spiritedly, "Then I don't like you. And I'll never come to your church anymore."

Having eliminated most of Hardy's Christian symbolism, Polanski explores images connected with paganism more sympathetically. He converts Angel into a Victorianized Pan figure, a seductive presence among the naiadic milkmaids at Talbothays, replete with flute and a leafy, chaplet-like headdress. (Hardy, by contrast, provides him with a small harp and has his wedding to Tess take place at Christmas.) Later, in a scene significantly altered from the novel, Tess puts her hand on a stone and prays in an attempt to change her fortunes. She is warned away by a passerby, who tells her that her gesture is more likely to bring her bad luck than good. Carrying a large basket with a goose in it, the old peasant looks like a figure out of a Mother Goose story, and his dire warning takes on the color of a folk superstition, like the earlier discussion at Talbothays about the butter failing to turn. Yet the old peasant's prediction is correct—as is the interpretation of Dairyman Crick's wife of the butter's failure to turn ("Someone's in love").

Polanski is drawn to the sense of magic that inspires religious invention, the attempt to make connections between the self and the world. His *Tess* alludes to a charming but outmoded way of life in which people create myths to grant themselves a meaningful place in the cosmos. In the film, such myths emerge more as expressions of imagination than of truth. They are closely related to art, and to suggest this connection Polanski has made the most of Hardy's tendency toward self-conscious artifice, conspicuously expressed in the painterly quality of both novel and film. Hardy's descriptions, reflecting a thorough knowledge of the painting of his day, often refer to artificial rather than natural models.[10] Such painterly references also play a central role in the film, as they did in Polanski's earlier *When Angels Fall*. There, as here, Polanski presents the world as an imaginative artistic construct of reality rather than as a direct, "truthful" representation of it.

In a general sense, the carefully orchestrated lighting and composition of many episodes present nature viewed through the prism of art (an approach prompting several reviewers to condemn the film as too picturesque). At the same time, more specific references allude to the work of particular nineteenth-century artists and movements: peasants out of Millet, Turneresque mists, skies reminiscent of Constable, Corot-like roads, a boat on a pond as Monet or Renoir might have seen it. Inspired by his source, Polanski has gone far beyond Hardy, not only in the emphasis he gives to painterly allusions but also in the scope of his references. Later in the film, the visual effects begin to suggest painters in the modern tradition. The scene at Angel's parents as well as those at Flintcomb-Ash are realized in a limited, cubist-like palette of grays and beiges, and the grainy fox-hunting incident suggests pointillism. In addition, the camera's contemplation of the threshing machine has futurist overtones. In these references to modernism, stylization and abstraction replace the harmonious interaction of human beings and nature characteristic of nineteenth-century realism and impressionism.

Hardy's novel refers to traditions not only in the visual arts but also in the narrative ones, by creating what Donald Davidson has called "a world like that of later balladry and folktale, from which old beliefs have receded, leaving a residue of the merely strange."[11] The balladic mode mimics a universe where narrative is closely allied with myth and magic. The archetypal outlines of the characters are suited to this spirit: Angel an inconstant prig; Alec a sybaritic parvenu; and Tess herself a strong, warm-blooded peasant. Polanski expresses these traits by means of traditional visual conventions: Alec's mustache, Angel's sudden, insubstantial movements, Tess's sensuous lower lip. These characters are not as highly individualized as they would be in a more rigorously realist narrative, and their emotions are expressed largely through musical motifs in lieu of individuating histrionics. Polanski modifies his source in such a way as to underlay the smoothly naturalistic surface of the story with an aura of quaint contrivance, creating a more subtle effect than the modernist stylization that characterizes most of his other films.

The progress of Hardy's narrative also reflects his interest in balladry. Extensive dramatic foreshadowing and a rigorous concatenation of events from the moment Jack Durbyfield learns of his lineage connote the old-fashioned teleological perspective associated with the ballad form. This deterministic vision of fate is, in turn, related to Hardy's religious preoccupations. In the novel, Tess is doomed by her presence on a "blighted" star (25) and by the curse on her family. This fate is related to the death of her family's horse Prince, and eventually, after an implacable series of consequences, her own.

For Polanski, however, the story's sense of doom grows not out of divine judgment or the sport of the gods, as is hinted in the novel, but rather from a vision of meaningless death as the ultimate conclusion of all human endeavor. The film omits references to the family curse or Prince's death, opting instead to foreshadow the heroine's fate in the opening scene, where an extraordinary long tracking shot connects the landscape, Tess's innocent pleasures, and her father, who crosses from another direction the road she and her companions have just danced by. The shot concludes as the camera turns back to observe Jack Durbyfield being hailed by Parson Tringham as "Sir John." This fluid movement indicates that the harmony between nature and humanity is the product of an aesthetic rather than a "realistic" vision. Tess's fate is foreshadowed by means of a stylistic motif rather than a more naturalistic incident in the plot. Nonetheless, Polanski's uncharacteristically sympathetic attitude toward his material can be seen in the contrast between this opening and the similarly long tracking shot that opens *The Tenant*, where our sense of the realistic wholeness of the environment is gradually subverted and fragmented by a descent into fantasy and paranoia.

Though Hardy's pessimism in the face of the Victorian faith in progress has often been noted, Polanski's narrative is even more closed and more rigidly gloomy than that of his source. Hardy mitigates the tragic conclusion of his story by including an exchange between Tess and Angel in which her question, "Do you think we shall meet again after we are dead?" remains unanswered by him, preserving a characteristically ambiguous glimmer of hope for a future in another world.[12] Polanski substitutes the question, "Do you think our souls will take flight together?" This question recalls an earlier exchange involving Tess's charmingly naive fancy about "our souls leaving our bodies" while gazing at the stars (327). In the film, then, her hope for a life after death is clearly an expression of ingenuous folk superstition.

If the film allows no hope for a better life in another world, neither does it allow hope for a better life in this one. Hardy's narrative concludes with Tess's sister Liza-Lu, a "spiritualized version" of the heroine herself, arriving to comfort Angel (329). We are even encouraged to think they could eventually marry. ("People do, occasionally, marry sister-in-laws," Tess hints [326].) Polanski, however, omits this reference as well. The film's final image reveals Tess and Angel walking away between two policemen on horseback as the final credit sequence announces her subsequent hanging. The shot completes the movement of Tess's initial appearance, when she was skipping toward us along another road, part of a bright, open composition that has become darkened and closed by the certainty of the end of her journey. Just before this picture, we hear faint echoes of the music from her May Day dance as the camera looks out from Stonehenge toward the rising sun, recalling the sunset of the opening dance sequence. It is a neat, formally elegant conclusion, but its closure is the product of directorial artifice. If Polanski's *Tess* explores a world in which human beings could feel connected with nature, it is a world we now can envision only as the creation of innocent illusion—or of art.

Society and Sexuality

Though *Tess* portrays the end of an innocent sense of emotional harmony between individuals and the world around them, it sees the possibility of such harmony more positively than any of Polanski's previous films. The center of this newly positive vision is Tess herself. Like the peasant girl in *When Angels Fall*, she is seduced and abandoned by a man above her station. And like Carol in *Repulsion*, the oppressive forces in her character and in her culture ultimately drive her to murder. But she is a richer, warmer character than either of these earlier figures, and she achieves a fulfillment denied to any of Polanski's other protagonists.

This fulfillment is sexual. In *Tess*, though the heroine is brutally and repeatedly victimized by the institutionalized sexual practices of her culture, the film emphasizes the beauty and validity of her own sexuality, which is envisioned as a desire to create bonds to others rather than to exert power over them. The men who desire her, by contrast, enact sexually oppressive codes of behavior that lead inevitably to her destruction, so that, at the film's conclusion, she becomes another of Polanski's victims. In the meantime, however, the film departs from the tone of Hardy's original novel to emphasize Tess's own sexuality, suggesting both the violation of Tess's sexual will and the nature of its fulfillment, a fulfillment based not on principles of dominance and submission but on nurture and need.

"Tess should be a film about intolerance," Polanski has said, "a very romantic story but at the same time very topical. This modern aspect was already present in Hardy. All we did was focus on it."[13] While a number of critics have seen *Tess of the D'Urbervilles* as a novel primarily concerned with the demise of the peasantry,[14] in the film the power struggle inherent in a changing class system becomes a power struggle centered on the quest for sexual dominance.

Of course, sexual oppression is an issue in Hardy's novel, too, as is evident in its subtitle, "A Pure Woman Faithfully Presented," as well as in Hardy's introductory remarks about his intention to tell a story "that begins where most leave off"—that is, after the sexual "fall" of his heroine. For Hardy, however, what was in question was the sexual double standard as defined by a repressive society. Polanski is more concerned with a woman's sexuality as central to her identity and with the social roles by which female sexuality is crushed and perverted.

For this reason the film minimizes the class conflict in the novel. All three of Hardy's major characters are social anomalies: Alec D'Urberville having a false title; Angel "lowering" himself to become a farmer; and Tess a member of a peasant family with an aristocratic lineage. Hardy takes pains to define the class of Tess's family and the misfortunes it causes them. After Jack Durbyfield's death, his widow and children are evicted from their home because it is wanted for tenant farmers rather than "liviers." Later Tess's status in society figures heavily in her prospective marriage. Angel Clare's family objects strenuously to his choice of a bride not of his class, and much is made of the fact that they do not attend his wedding. All of these details are omitted from the film. Polanski's cynical dismissal of class conflict is suggested by his portrayal of Angel. As a student of Marxism, Angel represents the prevalent form of twentieth-century social utopianism, but his commitment to an intellectual systemization of social processes blinds him to emotional truth.

Because the shifting class relationships in the novel are centered in the interactions among the three major characters, the rest of society remains "little more than accessories."[15] Conversely, in the film the secondary characters are painted with such vividness that they were seen by some reviewers as overwhelming the three main figures. Polanski's increased emphasis on social context, however, deflects interest from the issue of the class struggle by presenting society as warmer and more nurturing than in the novel. The engagingly obsequious old woman who takes care of Angel and Tess's honeymoon house at Wellbridge has been added, and both the dairymaid Marian and Angel's mother have become much more openly affectionate figures than those depicted by Hardy. Significantly, all of these are women; for Polanski's Tess, unlike Hardy's, is not victimized by society at large so much as she is by men.

Thus the film omits much of the novel's emphasis on society's condemnation of Tess's indiscretion. The embarrassment of her father after she returns home and the close questioning of Angel's mother about his wife's "virtue" do not appear in the film; nor does the ugly incident in which a man who recognizes Tess makes an insinuating remark to her in front of Angel just before the two are to be married. Moreover, Polanski includes

an obviously pregnant maiden at the May Day dance that opens the film—
the point evidently being that her condition is easily accepted in the society in which she and Tess move.

Though Tess emerges as less a victim in the film than in the book, Polanski, like Hardy before him, has been criticized for creating an overly
passive heroine.[16] To some extent, however, this aspect of her character
plays an essential part in the story's thrust: Tess's final resting place, on a
rock at Stonehenge, symbolizes her position as a social scapegoat. Polanski's Tess, however, actively searches for sexual fulfillment, and this, to
her, means a right to express her own sexual desires. Writing in the nineteenth century, Hardy could scarcely have understood such aspirations in
the same terms. As Elaine Showalter has shown, any expression of sexuality in women was looked on with extreme suspicion in Victorian England.
"Since overt sexuality was a symptom of many supposed categories of female insanity," Showalter notes, "its manifestation at any stage of the female life cycle could lead to incarceration even when no other symptoms
were present."[17] Thus Hardy's novel, though scandalous in its time, understandably deals with sexuality in conservative terms, avoiding any direct depiction of sexual activity. Polanski's narrative, by contrast,
emphasizes the revelation of sexual passion. And because of this new orientation, Tess is a more forceful presence in the film; for while Hardy's
heroine is probably seduced, Polanski's is certainly raped.

This change has far-reaching implications for both novel and film. With
the changes in sexual mores that have taken place over the past century,
stories of seduction, of which Hardy's *Tess* is one of the finest examples,
are no longer viable. For we are now more aware of the active sexual will
possessed by women. In speaking of the seduction story, Elizabeth Hardwick has pointed out that "when it is successful, we naturally look about
for a lack of resolution and resistance in the object; guile and insistence
are clever at uncovering pockets of complicity."[18] In the novel, we may
imagine such pockets of complicity in Tess. In the film, however, it is clear
that Alec violates her will; she desires only Angel.

Hardy treats sexuality solely in terms of power, of relationships built on
patriarchal prerogatives of class and gender. Thus Alec exploits Tess both
as a woman and as a peasant. In her relationship with Angel, however, she
is still the weaker, both socially inferior and intellectually enthralled. Hardy's narrator does not condemn her for her acceptance of this position.
The Angel of the novel is a more benevolent master than Alec D'Urberville; but he remains a master. His marriage is based on two premises:
Tess's submission and his willingness to educate her, socially and
intellectually.[19]

Polanski, by contrast, addresses himself to the perversion of sexual desire into sexual slavery, a major theme in all his work. Following the rape
scene, he adds a brief sequence showing the luxury Alec offers Tess, lux-

ury that she will reject. With this vignette, the film distinguishes her economic advantage from her sexual happiness. That Tess also understands this distinction is clear from her troubled expression, captured in close-up. The sequence begins with another close-up, this one of a new hat that Alec has bought his mistress. Tess's own, simpler hat had earlier served her well on the ride to Trantridge when she used it to help preserve her sexual independence. Later, the economic price she must pay for this sense of herself is symbolized by the appropriation of another article of clothing, her shoes, taken up by her rival Mercy Chant.

Tess's sexual independence, however, runs counter to a society that expects her, like Mercy, to barter her sexual allegiance for economic security. Joan Durbyfield assumes that her daughter will try to use her good looks to trap Alec into marriage. After Tess refuses to do this, she is accused by Farmer Grobey of being a "fancy woman," one who trades sexual favors for temporary rather than permanent monetary gain. Ultimately, Tess is forced to come to terms with this view, substituting lavish physical adornment for authentic sexual passion during her stay with Alec at Sandbourne. There, dressed in the elaborate negligee with which her lover has purchased her body, she sobs hopelessly over her broken marriage. Irritated by her continued emotional insubordination, he contemptuously asks her if she has "the vapours." She gazes at a knife resting on a plate of red meat and is reminded of Alec slicing meat with a similar implement during their first encounter. Having carelessly violated her body and spirit as though she were nothing more than a piece of meat, he ultimately encounters a more willful and open violence, which his actions have produced. By denying her identity, he has destroyed her empathy.

His guilt is shared by the audience, for in scenes between Alec and Tess Polanski's camera encourages us to view her body as Alec does, with prurient interest. Her mouth, especially, is treated in this way, most strikingly as she eats the strawberries Alec gives her and again when he teaches her to whistle. The heroine is therefore doubly victimized; and we experience her revenge as a reaction not only to Alec but also to the film text itself. The murder itself, however, is not shown, for Polanski is more concerned in this film about emphasizing the fragile interactions that bring people together rather than the violent schisms that tear them apart.

Tess's sexual fulfillment with Angel is more central to the film than her sexual oppression by Alec. Polanski shows Tess and Angel as equals. They are almost the same height, and the broad-shouldered Nastassia Kinski moves with a more masculine sense of authority than the puckish Peter Firth. There is also an aura of intellectual equality. The romance begins in the film when he is struck by the theory she espouses about the soul, whereas in the novel it is the "flutey" sound of her voice that first catches his attention. Moreover, Tess visually asserts her desire for Angel in the opening scene. After his brief participation in the May Day dance, Polan-

Tess with her lover and her husband, the two men who shape her fate. Courtesy of the Chicago Reader.

ski gives Tess her first close-up as her eyes follow his retreating figure. Their pairing thus has much in common with what Carolyn Heilbrun refers to as sexual androgyny.[20] In the film the couple's final erotic encounter provides a dramatic contrast to the earlier rape scene. In the former instance, Alec forces his victim to comply with his will by means of his superior strength. As he uses his body to pin her to the ground, Polanski's camera observes her helpless struggle from above: she is thereby trapped both by her seducer and by the camera itself, simultaneously a victim both of rape and of pornographic fetishism. If the audience's perversity is thereby enlisted and exposed, however, it is less aggressively attacked than in Polanski's other films. The spectators' role is here doubled in the look of Alec's horse, whose gaze constitutes a far less scurrilous comment on our motives than the gaping and sadistic crowds who observe the humiliations of Polanski's other protagonists. And later, in Tess's lovemaking scene with Angel, our relationship with her becomes more empathic than voyeuristic, for she is here portrayed more as an active force than a passive victim. Tess takes the initiative by raising Angel's head from her lap. As the two embrace and fall to the ground together, the camera's short tracking motions share in the circling movements by which each rolls over the other in a rhapsodic alternation of the positions of power and submission.

But if this moment is fulfilling, it is also illusory. Tess's rape is portrayed as part of nature. Set in a forest, it is accompanied by the cacophonous chirping of birds—foreshadowing Tess's frenzied, birdlike movements as she tries to rebuff Alec. The scene ends as a mist clouds her suffering. Her scene with Angel, by contrast, is marked by artifice. It occurs indoors rather than outside, and the soundtrack features the asynchronic harmonies of Phillip Sarde's orchestral score. The stylized image of Tess herself as a "scarlet woman," in her red dress and frizzled hair, carries overtones of a Toulouse-Lautrec poster.

Instead of mist, the scene ends as the camera tracks into a stained-glass window depicting a medieval town, a clear reference to pre-Raphaelite painting. As a precursor to the symbolist movement, pre-Raphaelitism foreshadowed modernism, setting the tone for the alienation of the individual from nature and society and the consequent mood of fragmentation, stylization, and despair that has characterized much of the art of our own time.[21] Both incandescent and aestheticized, Polanski's image of the stained-glass window also includes the shadows of birds fruitlessly beating their wings against the pane: art veiling and imprisoning nature even as it reveals it. His own art, the film itself, has also given us only the shadows of living forms, balancing the momentary epiphanies of intimacy against the enduring illusions of art. In contrast to his earlier depictions of art in terms of the perverse antagonism it may foster between exhibitionistic artists and voyeuristic spectators, this image defines art as the benign creation of a world of desire shared by artist and audience.

By the end of the film Tess has become a stylized "scarlet woman." Courtesy of the Chicago Reader.

This climactic love scene does not appear in the novel, and it points to the different visions of the two artists. For Hardy, the central issue of the story is justice; for Polanski, it is erotic fulfillment. This difference stems, at least in part, from the different times in which the two works were composed. Looking toward the future, Hardy is disheartened but also uncertain—about the fate of the individual and of society as a whole. Polanski, who has experienced a future Hardy could only envision, believes that the only salvation is a private and aesthetic one, and that even this was only possible in the past.

By returning to the past, Polanski has rediscovered in *Tess* a hope for the future of his own art. It is, to be sure, tentative, momentary, and subjective. Portrayed in a subtly mannered way that calls its relationship to the real world into question, this hope is symbolized by the momentary pleasure of the erotic encounter. *Tess* celebrates the feeling of harmony—however illusory—which people can feel for one another—and which, by analogy, enables artists and audiences to share in the pleasure of created beauty. In this film, Polanski has for the first time expressed in an ingenuous way his affection for his characters and for his craft. Here style does not simply comment on substance; it enhances it.

The view of sexual fulfillment and aesthetic harmony portrayed in *Tess* minimizes the role of society. Yet Polanski could not have come to such a vision without having first explored the popular realist tradition. By examining in his commercial films social and psychological oppression, especially of women, which engendered the nihilism of his early modernist projects, he was able, in *Tess*, to envision mature sexual expression.

The past Polanski has returned to in *Tess* is, in a sense, his own; for in this film he examines the artistic roots of his early modernist background in postwar Poland. After a career marked by an extraordinary capacity to capitalize on both cultural and aesthetic disorientation, he has "come back from the other side," as he once suggested he might. This circuitous journey could represent a cycle that he will continue to repeat in future projects, thereby enacting in the pattern of his own career the motif of the endless repetitions that characterize the structure of his films. On the other hand, *Tess* could signal the beginning of a more optimistic and progressive vision. "Until *Tess*," the director has said, "I had never had the impression of making the film that corresponded exactly to my deepest feelings. *Tess* is that film. *Tess* is 'my' film, the film of my mature years."[22]

Notes and References

Chapter One

1. Harrison Engle, "Polanski in New York," *Film Comment*, Fall 1968, p. 89.
2. Morse Peckham, *Man's Rage for Chaos* (New York: Schocken, 1975), p. 314.
3. Gene Moskowitz, "The Uneasy East: Aleksander Ford and the Polish Cinema," *Sight and Sound*, Winter 1957–58, p. 137.
4. Mira and Antonin Liehm, *The Most Important Art: Eastern European Film After 1945* (Berkeley: University of California Press, 1977), p. 112.
5. Ibid., p. 375.
6. Polanski prefers to call his film by its British title, *Dance of the Vampires*, rather than *The Fearless Vampire Killers*, the title under which it was originally released in the United States. My own references to the film here use this title also.
7. Joseph Gelmis, *The Film Director as Superstar* (Garden City, N.Y,.: Doubleday, 1970), p. 149.
8. Accounts of Polanski's early years can be found in Thomas Kiernan's *The Roman Polanski Story* (New York, 1980), and Barbara Leaming's *Polanski: The Filmmaker as Voyeur* (New York, 1982). Polanski himself has recently recalled these experiences in his autobiography, *Roman* (New York: William Morrow, 1984). Though the autobiography appeared too late to be used as a source for my own work, it does not significantly contradict the facts or arguments offered here.
9. Joel Reisner and Bruce Kane, "An Interview with Roman Polanski," *Cinema* (Los Angeles) 5, no. 2:12.
10. Quoted in David Middleton, "The Self-Reflexive Nature of Polanski's *Macbeth*," *University of Dayton Review* 14, no. 1 (Winter 1979–80):90.
11. Larry DuBois, "The *Playboy* Interview: Roman Polanski," *Playboy*, December 1971, p. 118.
12. Daniel Gerould, *Twentieth Century Polish Avant-Garde Drama* (Ithaca, N.Y.: Cornell University Press, 1977), p. 13.
13. Ibid.
14. See Tymon Terlecki, ed., *Polish Historical Antecedents to Surrealism in Drama* (Wroclow, 1973); and Harold B. Segal, ed., *Polish Romantic Drama* (Ithaca, N.Y.: Cornell University Press, 1977).

15.   For a description of this relationship, see Martin Esslin, *The Theatre of the Absurd* (Garden City, N.Y.: Doubleday, 1969), pp. 343–45.
16.   Ibid., p. 272.
17.   See Gerould, *Twentieth Century*, p. 88; and Ronald Hayman, *Theater and Anti-Theater: New Movements Since Beckett* (New York: Oxford University Press, 1979), p. 223.
18.   Jerzy Grotowski, *Toward a Poor Theater* (New York: Touchstone/Simon & Schuster, 1968), p. 8.
19.   Ibid., p. 20.
20.   Gerould, *Twentieth Century*, p. 77.
21.   Alistair Whyte, *New Cinema in Eastern Europe* (London: Studio Vista; New York: Dutton, 1971), p. 7.
22.   See Michael Jon Stoil, *Cinema Beyond the Danube: The Camera and Politics* (Metuchen, N.J.: Scarecrow Press, 1974), p. 67.
23.   Quoted in Liehm and Liehm, *Most Important Art*, p. 178.
24.   See Michael Delahaye and Jean-Andre Fieschi, "Landscape of a Mind: Interview with Roman Polanski," in Roman Polanski, *Three Film Scripts* (London: Lorrimer, 1975), p. 209. A thorough analysis of the role of genre painting in the film's complex narrative structure has been carried out in Jerry W. Carlson's paper "Visual Style as Narrative Voice: The Example of *When Angels Fall*," delivered at the 1979 Modern Language Association convention.
25.   "Wajda-Polanski: faire des films en Pologne ou ailleurs," *Jeune Cinéma* 91 (December 1975):13. Reprinted from *Kino* 7, no. 2 (February 1972). Translation from Polish to French by J.-C. Kociolek and D. Nicaise; translation from French to English by the author.

Chapter Two

1.   Because of the continuing debate about the issue of modernism and what is often called postmodernism, I have not tried here to distinguish between them; instead, I have used the blanket term "modernism" to refer to what may be two very different traditions. To trace the origins of Polanski's own style, I have emphasized its relationship to two particular schools within this larger movement, surrealism and the theater of the absurd, which have clear and well-documented historical and theoretical associations.
2.   Georg Lukács, *The Meaning of Contemporary Realism* (London: Merlin Press, 1963), p. 21.
3.   Susan Sontag, *Against Interpretation* (New York: Delta, 1966), p. 20.
4.   See Reisner and Kane, "Interview," p. 12; Claude Sauderman, "An Interview with Roman Polanski," *Seventh Art* 2, no. 1 (Winter 1963):8; Wajda, "Wajda-Polanski," p. 13; Mitch Tuchman, "Exiled on Main Street," *Village Voice*, July 26, 1976, p. 108; and Joseph Gelmis, *The Film Director as Superstar* (Garden City, N.Y.: Doubleday, 1970), p. 149. An excellent brief analysis of these influences can be found in Colin McArthur's "Polanski," *Sight and Sound* 38, no. 1 (Winter 1968–69):14–17.
5.   Reisner and Kane, "Interview," p. 12.
6.   See Leo Brandy, *The World in a Frame* (Garden City, N.Y.: Doubleday, 1977), p. 47.

7. Ivan Butler, *The Cinema of Roman Polanski* (New York: A. S. Barnes; London: A. Zwemmer, 1970), p. 93.

8. Gordon Gow, "Satisfaction: A Most Unpleasant Feeling," *Films and Filming* 15, no. 7 (April 1969):18.

9. N. S. Litowitz and K. M. Newman, "Borderline Personality and the Theater of the Absurd," *Archives of General Psychiatry*, March 16, 1967, pp. 268–80. Christopher Lasch has extended a similar analysis of absurdist theater to apply to the culture as a whole in *The Culture of Narcissism* (New York: Warner Books, 1979), pp. 159–65.

10. Quoted in Esslin, *Theatre of the Absurd*, p. 275.

11. Reisner and Kane, "Interview," p. 12.

12. Eugene Ionesco, *Notes and Counter Notes*, tr. Donald Watson (New York: French and European Books, 1964), pp. 80–81.

13. Noted by Roy Armes in *The Ambiguous Image* (Bloomington: Indiana University Press, 1976), p. 177.

14. A. Artaud, "The Theater of Cruelty (First Manifesto)," in *The Theater and Its Double*, tr. Mary Caroline Richards (New York: Grove press, 1958), p. 92.

15. Reisner and Kane, "Interview," p. 11.

16. Engle, "Polanski in New York," p. 9.

17. Maurice Nadean, *History of Surrealism*, tr. Richard Howard (New York: MacMillan, 1965), p. 185.

18. *Sight and Sound*, Winter 1968–69, p. 15.

19. See especially Leaming, *Polanski*, and Jane Marcus, "A *Tess* for Child Molesters," *Jump/Cut*, no. 26 (Winter 1982):7.

20. Bernard Weinraub, "A Visit with Roman Polanski," *New York Times Magazine*, December 12, 1971, p. 72.

21. James Leach, "Notes on Polanski's Cinema of Cruelty," *Wide Angle*, 7, no. 1 (1978):32–39.

22. André Breton, *Manifestoes of Surrealism*, tr. Richard Seaver and Helen R. Lane (Ann Arbor: University of Michigan Press, 1977), p. 14.

23. Christopher Williams, *Realism and the Cinema* (London: Routledge & Kegan Paul, 1981), p. 180. For an excellent brief discussion of filmic realism see Roy Armes, "Realism and the Cinema," in his *Patterns of Realism* (Cranbury, N.J.: A. S. Barnes; London: A. Zwemmer, 1971), pp. 17–22.

24. Quoted in Nadeau, *History of Surrealism*, p. 184.

25. Delahaye and Fieschi, "Landscape of a Mind," p. 213.

26. See especially Engle, "Polanski in New York," p. 5; and *AFI Dialogue on Film/Roman Polanski*, pp. 8–9, 22–23.

27. Delahaye and Fieschi, "Landscape of a Mind," p. 209.

28. Gelmis, *Film Director*, p. 149.

29. DuBois, "*Playboy* Interview," p. 108.

30. Gelmis, *Film Director*, p. 146.

31. DuBois, "*Playboy* Interview," p. 118.

32. Engle, "Polanski in New York," p. 7.

33. *AFI Dialogue on Film*, p. 10.

34. Gow, "Satisfaction," p. 16.

35. DuBois, "*Playboy* Interview," p. 114.

36. Gelmis, *Film Director*, p. 148.

37.   Ibid., p. 209.

38.   Delahaye and Fieschi, "Landscape of a Mind," pp. 207–8.

39.   Gelmis, p. 145.

40.   Gow, p. 18.

41.   Gelmis, p. 145.

42.   Raymond Durgnat, review of *The Fat and the Lean*, *Films and Filming*, May 1971, p. 97.

43.   *Three Film Scripts*, pp. 209, 213.

44.   Some of these Soviet-bloc reviews are annotated in *Roman Polanski: A Guide to References and Resources*, ed. Virginia Wright Wexman and Gretchen Bisplinghoff (Boston: 1979). See entries 54, 66, 70, 78, and 80.

45.   See Renee Ford, "Interpretation," *New York Times*, November 17, 1963, sec. 2, p. 9, for Polanski's own statement of this.

46.   David S. Hall, *Film Society Review*, January 1965, p. 14.

47.   Northrop Frye, *The Anatomy of Criticism* (New York: Atheneum, 1969), p. 163.

48.   Polanski has objected to attempts to read such symbolic meanings into this film. See Dr. Donald J. Marcuse, "Mailed Opinion," *New York Times*, November 17, 1963, sec. 2, p. 9; and Bosley Crowther, "Exposing the Obscure," *New York Times*, November 10, 1963, sec. 2, p. 1. For Polanski's response, see Ford, "Interpretations," p. 9. The debate is summarized in Herman Weinberg's "Basic Drama Is Two," in his *Saint Cinema* (New York: Drama Book Specialists, 1970), pp. 231–32.

49.   This aspect of the film was stressed in Vernon Young's review, which is reprinted in his *On Film* (Chicago: Quadrangle, 1972), pp. 366–68.

50.   Sybil March, *"Knife in the Water," Seventh Art* 2, no. 1 (Winter 1973):6.

51.   *AFI Dialogue on Film*, p. 11.

52.   Andy Warhol, "Andy Warhol Tapes Roman Polanski," *Interview*, no. 38 (November 1973):11.

53.   Gelmis, *Film Director*, p. 148.

54.   Ibid.

55.   Reisner and Kane, "Interview," p. 12.

56.   In Robert Corrigan, ed., *Tragedy: Vision and Form*, (Chicago: Science Research Associates; San Francisco: Chandler, 1965), p. 245.

57.   Jack Shadoian, *Dreams and Dead Ends: The American Gangster Crime Film* (Cambridge: MIT Press, 1972), p. 3.

58.   See John G. Cawelti, *Adventure, Mystery and Romance* (Chicago: University of Chicago Press, 1976), pp. 41–42.

59.   Tom Milne, *"Cul-de-Sac," Sight and Sound*, Summer 1966, p. 147.

60.   Warhol, "Andy Warhol," p. 12.

61.   *New York Times*, April 4, 1974, p. 13.

62.   Leaming, *Polanski*, p. 147.

63.   *AFI Dialogue on Film*, p. 6.

64.   Reisner and Kane, "Interview," p. 12; and Ford, "Interpretation," p. 9.

Chapter Three

1.   Paul D. Zimmerman, "Blood and Water," *Newsweek*, July 1, 1974, p. 94.

2. Laura Mulvey, "Visual Pleasure and Narrative Cinema," *Screen* 16 (Autumn 1975):9.

3. Robin Wood, "An Introduction to the American Horror Film," in Robin Wood and Richard Lippe, eds., *American Nightmare: Essays on the Horror Film* (Toronto: Festival of Festivals, 1979), p. 9.

4. The classic essay relating popular horror legends to psychological disturbances is Sigmund Freud's "The Uncanny," in *Standard Edition of the Complete Psychological Works*, 17:217–252. This essay inspired other such studies, most importantly Ernest Jones's *On the Nightmare* (New York: Liveright, 1971) and Otto Rank's *The Double*, tr. Harry Tucker (Chapel Hill: University of North Carolina Press, 1971).

5. David Punter, *The Literature of Terror* (London: Longman, 1980), p. 419. Other useful recent discussions of the genre include Norman Holland and Leona Sherman, "Gothic Possibilities," *New Literary History* 8 (1976–77):279–94; Ellen Moers, *Literary Women* (Garden City, N.Y.: Doubleday, 1977); Elizabeth MacAndrew, *The Gothic Tradition in Fiction* (New York: Columbia University Press, 1979); and Judith Wilt, *Ghosts of the Gothic* (Princeton, N.J.: Princeton University Press, 1981).

6. See Gerard Lenne, "Monster and Victim: Women in the Horror Film," tr. Elayne Donenberg and Thomas Agabite, in Patricia Erens, ed., *Sexual Stratagems* (New York: Horizon, 1979), pp. 31–40, for a discussion of the ways in which Polanski's horror films manipulate this convention.

7. Punter, *Literature of Terror*, p. 95.

8. Tzvetan Todorov, *The Fantastic: A Structural Approach to a Literary Genre*, tr. Richard Howard (Ithaca, N.Y.: Cornell University Press, 1975).

9. Such regressed modes have become the focus of considerable interest within the psychoanalytic community in recent years. Useful discussions can be found in Heinz Kohut, *The Analysis of the Self* (New York: International University Press, 1971) and *The Restoration of the Self* (New York: International University Press, 1977); Otto Kernberg, *Borderline Conditions and Pathological Narcissism* (New York: Aronson, 1975); R. D. Laing, *The Divided Self* (Harmondsworth, Middlesex, England: Penguin, 1969), which I use most extensively in this chapter; and Jacques Lacan, "The Mirror Stage as Formative of the Function of the I as Revealed in Psychoanalytic Experience," in *Ecrits*, tr. Alan Sheridan (New York: W. W. Norton, 1977), pp. 93–100. Lacan is a particularly relevant figure here because of his early ties with the surrealist group. For a discussion of this relationship see Linda Williams, *Figures of Desire: A Theory and Analysis of Surrealist Film* (Chicago and Urbana: University of Illinois Press, 1981), pp. 43–45.

10. For a discussion of the way techniques of the horror film reproduce unconscious wishes, see Dennis L. White, "The Poetics of Horror: More Than Meets the Eye," *Cinema Journal* 10 (Spring 1971):1–18.

11. T. J. Ross, "*Repulsion* and the New Mythology," *Film Heritage* 4, no. 2 (Winter 1968–69):9. A similar point is made by Susan Sontag, who comments on the use of insanity among contemporary artists as a means of opening up the dramatic representation "to levels of experience which are more heroic, more rich in fantasy, more philosophical." *Against Interpretation*, p. 169.

12. Delahaye and Fieschi, "Landscape of a Mind," p. 213.

13. Harlan Ellison, "The Three Faces of Fear," *Cinema* (Los Angeles) 3, no. 2 (March 1966):14.

14.   Gerard Brach, "Polanski Via Brach," *Cinéma* 65 (Paris), no. 93 (1965):27.

15.   Leaming, *Polanski*, pp. 66–67.

16.   Roy Armes, *The Ambiguous Image* (Bloomington: Indiana University Press, 1976), p. 177. Other critics considered the film a direct imitation of Hitchcock. See Hollis Alpert, "The Headstrong Directors," *Saturday Review*, October 16, 1965, p. 63; and Brendan Gill, "Many Sufferers," *New Yorker*, October 9, 1965, p. 190.

17.   Critics who made such objections include Judith Crist, "Idle Dreams about Idols," in *The Private Eye, the Cowboy, and the Very Naked Girl* (New York: Holt, Rinehart & Winston, 1968), pp. 194–97; Bruce Stewart, "Excelsior: Roman Polanski," *Month* 41 (May 1969):307–9; Stanley Kauffmann, "End of an Epoch," *New Republic*, October 16, 1965, pp. 31–32; "A Maiden Berserk," *Time*, October 8, 1968, p. 115; and Peter John Dyer, "Repulsion," *Sight and Sound*, Summer 1965, p. 146.

18.   Delahaye and Fieschi, "Landscape of a Mind," p. 207.

19.   The role of society is also emphasized in Peter von Bagh's review of the film, though von Bagh finds it "never fully understood." See "Repulsion," *Movie* 14 (Autumn 1965):27–28. A similar objection is made in Neil Feinemann's discussion of *Repulsion* in *Persistence of Vision: The Films of Robert Altman* (New York: Arno Press, 1978), pp. 78–80.

20.   *Three Film Scripts*, p. 214.

21.   The sexual implications of women being granted the power of looking in films has been discussed in Linda Williams's "When the Woman Looks . . . ," in Linda Williams, Patricia Mellencamp, and Mary Ann Doane, eds., *Re-Vision: Feminist Essays in Film* (Los Angeles: American Film Institute and University Presses of America, 1983), pp. 53–67.

22.   Ross, "Repulsion," p. 1.

23.   Anon, "Repulsion," in Peter Cowie, ed., *International Film Guide 1966* (New York: Zoetrope; London: Tantivy, 1966), p. 84. Other appraisals that took a similar tack include Andrew Sarris, "Repulsion, The Ipcress File, The Hours of Love," *Village Voice*, October 7, 1965, p. 27; Charles Barr, "Repulsion," *Movie* 14 (Autumn 1965):26–27; Peter John Dyer, "Repulsion," *Sight and Sound*, Summer 1965, p. 146; and Colin McArthur, "Polanski," *Sight and Sound*, Winter 1968, p. 202.

24.   Punter, *Literature of Terror*, p. 368.

25.   For Polanski's statements of his complaints, see especially *AFI Dialogue on Film/Roman Polanski*, p. 9. The uncut version, released in the United States in 1980, was praised in a review by Andrew Sarris. See "Where Have All the Genres Gone," *Village Voice*, April 7, 1980, p. 37.

26.   Gow, "Satisfaction," p. 19.

27.   Barrie Pattison, *The Seal of Dracula* (London: Crown, 1975), p. 59. Quoted in Michael J. Murphy, *The Celluloid Vampires* (Ann Arbor, 1979), p. 116. A discussion of the influence of the Hammer films can be found in James Ursini and Alain Silver, *The Vampire Film* (Cranbury, N.J.: A. S. Barnes; London: A. Zwemmer, 1975), pp. 123–24.

28.   Butler, *Cinema of Roman Polanski*, pp. 131–32.

29.   For a discussion of this pattern, see Noel Carroll, "Nightmare and the

Horror Film: The Symbolic Biology of Fantastic Beings," *Film Quarterly* 34, no. 3 (Spring 1981):20. Anna Lawton's essay "The Double: A Doestoevskian Theme in Polanski," *Literature/Film Quarterly* 9, no. 11 (1981):121–29, develops a similar doubling motif in the film by opposing Alfred and the Professor as "two halves of a non-integrated personality."

30. The film's treatment of its Jewish characters has been criticized as anti-Semitic. See especially Butler, *Cinema of Roman Polanski*, p. 135, and Hollis Alpert, "The Fearless Vampire Killers," *Saturday Review*, November 25, 1967, p. 58.

31. DuBois, "*Playboy* Interview," p. 108.

32. For a fuller discussion of this phenomenon see Charles Derry, *Dark Dreams* (Cranbury, N.J.: A. S. Barnes; London: A. Zwemmer, 1977), pp. 92–97.

33. Engle, "Polanski in New York," p. 5.

34. See especially Butler, *Cinema of Roman Polanski*, p. 160; and Robert Chappetta, "*Rosemary's Baby*," *Film Quarterly* 22, no. 3 (Spring 1969):35–38.

35. Ellen Moers, *Literary Women* (Garden City, N.Y.: Doubleday, 1977), p. 142.

36. Reviewers who commented on the importance of this aspect of the film include Andrew Sarris, "*Rosemary's Baby*," *Village Voice*, July 25, 1968, p. 37; Henry Hart, "*Rosemary's Baby*," *Films in Review* 19, no. 9 (August-September 1968):456–57; and Penelope Gilliatt, "The Chaos of Cool," *New Yorker*, June 15, 1968, pp. 87–89.

37. Jones, *On the Nightmare*, p. 46. A similar observation has been made by Todorov in *The Fantastic:* "Desire, as a sensual temptation, finds its incarnation in several of the most common figures of the supernatural world, and most especially in the form of the Devil" (p. 127).

38. See Chappetta "*Rosemary's Baby*"; Stanley Solomon, *Beyond Formula* (New York: Harcourt Brace Jovanovich, 1976), pp. 149–52; and Marsha Kinder and Beverle Houston, "*Rosemary's Baby*," *Sight and Sound*, Winter 1978, pp. 17, 26.

39. Many of the techniques by which this effect is achieved are analyzed in Kinder and Houston's essay on the film.

40. Some reviewers complained about this aspect of the film. See especially Philip Hartung, "*Rosemary's Baby*," *Commonweal*, June 14, 1968, pp. 384–85.

41. This point was made by many reviewers. See Tom Milne, "*Le Locataire (The Tenant)*," *Monthly Film Bulletin*, September 1976, p. 193; Andrew Sarris, "Horrors! The World Is Coming to an End," *Village Voice*, July 12, 1976, p. 115; Jonathan Rosenbaum, "*The Tenant*," *Sight and Sound*, Autumn 1976, p. 263; Dilys Powell, "The Edge of Horror," *London Times*, August 27, 1976, p. 26; Richard Combs, "Conspiracy of Horrors," *London Times*, September 3, 1976, p. 7; and Colin Westerbeck, Jr., "The Screen," *Commonweal*, August 27, 1976, pp. 563–64.

42. Polanski's dual role as actor and director here is discussed in A. Alvarez, "Can Polanski Make a Star of Polanski," *New York Times*, February 22, 1976, sec. 2, pp. 1, 15; and David Overbey, "Polanski as Actor," *Sight and Sound*, Spring 1976, p. 84.

43. For a discussion of the relationship of transvestism to the quest for male dominance in modern fiction, see Sandra Gilbert's "Costumes of the Mind: Transvestism as Metaphor in Modern Literature," *Critical Inquiry* 7 (Winter

1980):391–417. Some of the film's reviewers objected to the "self-indulgence" of Polanski's portrayal of transvestism. See especially Frank Rich, *"The Tenant," New York Post,* June 21, 1976, p. 20; and Janet Maslin, "Jump!" *Newsweek,* June 28, 1976, p. 78.

44. This point was well made in Penelope Gilliatt's review of the film. See "Only a Lodger," *New Yorker,* July 5, 1976, p. 62.

45. Several reviewers complained of the awkward dubbing procedures. See especially Judith Crist, "Schtick by Simon, Paranoia by Polanski," *Saturday Review,* July 24, 1976, pp. 42–43; John Simon, "Untenable *Tenant,*" *New York Magazine,* June 28, 1976, pp. 66–68; and Robert Hatch, "Films," *Nation,* July 17, 1976, p. 60. The French version of the film reversed the dubbing procedure, giving rise to similar objections among the French reviewers. See Rosenbaum, *"The Tenant."*

46. A similar observation has been made by Linda Williams, whose essay on the film advances many of the same points made here. See "Film Madness: The Uncanny Return of the Repressed in Polanski's *The Tenant," Cinema Journal* 20 (Spring 1981):63–73.

Chapter Four

1. Larry DuBois, *"Playboy* Interview," p. 96.
2. Ibid., p. 97.
3. Ibid., p. 96.
4. Quoted in David Middleton, "The Self-Reflexive Nature of Polanski's *Macbeth," University of Dayton Review* 14, no. 1 (Winter 1979–80):90. For other interviews in which Polanski defends the film's authenticity see DuBois, *"Playboy* Interview"; and *"Macbeth* by Daylight," *Time,* January 25, 1971, p. 45.
5. Middleton, "Self-Reflexive," p. 92.
6. Terence St. John Marner, *Film Design* (Cranbury, N.J.: A. S. Barnes; London: A. Zwemmer, 1974), p. 135.
7. Frank Kermode, "Shakespeare in the Movies," *New York Review of Books,* May 4, 1972, p. 19.
8. *AFI Dialogue on Film/Roman Polanski,* p. 13.
9. DuBois, *"Playboy* Interview," p. 98.
10. Lynda Bundtzen, "The Rhetoric of the Unconscious: Shakespeare's *Macbeth,*" unpublished doctoral dissertation, University of Chicago, 1974, p. 340.
11. See *New Republic,* January 1, 1971, p. 22.
12. John Reddington, "Film, Play, and Idea," *Literature/Film Quarterly* 1 (Fall 1973):369. For analyses of the film that discuss its relationship to Kott see especially William Johnson, *"Macbeth," Film Quarterly* 25 (Spring 1972):41–48; Norman Berlin, *"Macbeth:* Polanski and Shakespeare," *Literature/Film Quarterly* 1 (Fall 1973):291–98. Kenneth S. Rothwell, "Roman Polanski's *Macbeth:* Golgotha Triumphant," *Literature/Film Quarterly* 1 (January 1973):71–75; and Jack Jorgens, *Shakespeare on Film* (Bloomington: Indiana University Press, 1977), pp. 161–74. By contrast, Nigel Andrews objects that the film fails by not offering a "committed interpretation" of the play. *"Macbeth," Sight and Sound,* Spring 1972, p. 108.

13. Jan Kott, *Shakespeare Our Contemporary* (New York: W. W. Norton, 1974), p. 86.

14. Ibid., p. 96.

15. The importance of the Macbeths' sexual relationship to the interpretation of the film has been stressed by Roger Manvell, *Theater and Film* (Cranbury, N.J., and London, 1979), pp. 154–64; and Gordon Gow, "*Macbeth,*" *Films and Filming* 18, no. 7 (April 1972):53–54.

16. Marner, *Film Design*, p. 30.

17. Ibid.

Chapter Five

1. Andrew Sarris, "Chinatown and Polanski-Towne: Tilting toward Tragedy," *Village Voice*, November 7, 1974, p. 85.

2. See *AFI Dialogue on Film/Roman Polanski*, pp. 10–11; and John Alonzo, "Behind the Scenes of Chinatown," *American Cinematographer*, May 1975, pp. 526–29, 564–65, 572–73, 585–91.

3. For further information about personality clashes during the making of the film see Tom Burke, "The Restoration of Roman Polanski," *Rolling Stone*, July 18, 1974, pp. 40–46; Mel Gussow, "Only Faye Dunaway Knows What She's Hiding," *New York Times*, October 20, 1974, sec. 2, pp. 1, 17, 19; and Martin Kasindorf, "Hot Writer," *Newsweek*, October 14, 1974, p. 114.

4. *AFI Dialogue on Film/Roman Polanski*, p. 2.

5. Ibid., p. 4.

6. Robert Towne, "Bogart and Belmondo: Where It Was and Where It's At," *Cinema* (Los Angeles), n.d., pp. 5–7.

7. See P. Cook, "The Sound Track," *Films in Review*, November 1974, pp. 560–63.

8. Roy M. Prendergast, *Film Music: A Neglected Art* (New York: W. W. Norton, 1977), p. 159.

9. See Hollis Alpert, "Jack, the Private Eye," *Saturday Review/World*, July 27, 1974, p. 46; and Burke, "Restoration of Roman Polanski," pp. 40–46.

10. See Kasindorf, "Hot Writer"; John Tuska, *The Detective in Hollywood* (Garden City, N.Y., 1978), p. 405; and Pauline Kael, "Beverly Hills as a Big Red," *New Yorker*, February 17, 1975, p. 92.

11. Alonzo, "Behind the Scenes," p. 528.

12. Raymond Chandler, *The Simple Art of Murder* (New York: Ballantine, 1972), p. 16.

13. John Cawelti, "*Chinatown* and Generic Transformation in Recent American Films," in *Film Theory and Criticism*, ed. Gerald Mast and Marshall Cohen (New York, 1979), p. 572.

14. Alonzo, "Behind the Scenes," p. 564.

15. Ibid., p. 573.

16. Artaud, *Theatre and Its Double*, p. 123.

17. Alonzo, "Behind the Scenes," p. 564.

18. No such incident is included in Hawks's film version, though Hawks appears to have shot it. See Roger Shatzkin, "Who Cares Who Killed Owen Tay-

lor?," in *The Modern American Novel and the Movies* (New York: Ungar, 1978), p. 86.

19.   Garrett Stewart, *"The Long Goodbye* from *Chinatown," Film Quarterly* 28, no. 2 (Winter 1974–75):25–32.

20.   Barbara Halpern Martineau's *"Chinatown's* Sexism," *Jump/Cut* 4 (November-December 1974):24, points out that certain male critics have ignored *Chinatown's* emphasis on women.

21.   See Herbert J. Gans, *"Chinatown:* An Anti-Capitalist Murder Mystery," *Social Policy* 5 (November-December 1974):48–49; James Kavanagh, *"Chinatown:* Other Places, Other Times," *Jump/Cut* 3 (September-October 1974):1, 8; and Murray Sperber, "Do as Little as Possible: Polanski's Message and Manipulation," *Jump/Cut* 3 (September-October 1974):9–10; and Pascal Kane, "La ville des feintes *(Chinatown)," Cahiers du Cinéma,* no. 256 (February-March 1975);63–64.

22.   William Kahrl, *Water and Power: The Conflict over Los Angeles' Water Supply in the Owens Valley* (Berkeley: University of California Press, 1982), p. 1. William Walling's review of the film in *Society,* November-December 1974, pp. 73–77, approaches it in terms of this political background.

23.   Kahrl, *Water and Power,* p. 18.

24.   Ibid., p. 20.

25.   Hayden White, *Metahistory: The Historical Imagination in Nineteenth-Century Europe* (Baltimore and London: Johns Hopkins University Press, 1973), p. 2.

26.   For a fuller discussion of this last analogy, see W. D. McGinnis, *"Chinatown:* Roman Polanski's Contemporary Oedipus Story," *Literature/Film Quarterly* 3, no. 3 (Summer 1975):249–51, and R. Barton Palmer, *"Chinatown* and the Detective Story," *Literature/Film Quartery* 5, no. 2 (Spring 1977):112–17. Deborah Linderman's essay "Oedipus in Chinatown," *Enclitic* 5 (Fall 1981):190–203, cleverly relates the Oedipus motif to the oedipal nature of the film's narrative considered from a Freudian perspective. In this view, the story reproduces in a disguised form the oedipal drive to discover the primal scene and to disclaim sexual difference. Linderman sees *Chinatown* as a "limit text" in that it posits incest as its narrative "secret," thereby threatening to explode the repressions that have motivated its production. But in her view Polanski's film ultimately stays within the limit by mystifying female sexuality and victimizing its major female character. The hero's growing impotence is attributed to his alliance with the feminine principle following Evelyn Mulwray's confession. My own argument, by contrast, attributes Gittes's failure to masculine patterns rather than feminine ones. His misplaced loyalty to these patterns leads him into difficulties both before Evelyn's confession (in the scene outside Katherine's hideout where his mysogyny prevents him from trusting Evelyn) and after it (when his sense of bravado leads him to stage a showdown with Noah Cross).

27.   For a good brief discussion of how the visual codes of realism operate in film see Colin MacCabe, "Realism and the Cinema: Notes on some Brechtian Themes," *Screen* 15, no. 2 (Summer 1974):7–17 (reprinted in *Realism and the Cinema,* ed. Christopher Williams [London: Routledge & Kegan Paul, 1980], pp. 152–162).

28.   Michel Foucault, *The Order of Things* (New York: Vintage, 1973), p. 219.

Chapter Six

1. Mitchell Glazer, "On the Lam with Roman Polanski," *Rolling Stone*, April 20, 1981, p. 44.
2. Aljean Harmetz, in *New York Times*, December 11, 1980, p. 69.
3. Joel Reisner and Bruce Kane, "An Interview with Roman Polanski," *Cinema* (Los Angeles) 5, no. 2 (n.d.):12.
4. For reviews that emphasized the film's uninspired fidelity to the novel, see especially Graham Smith, "Tess the Demure," *Times Literary Supplement*, September 12, 1980; William V Costanzo, "Polanski in Wessex Filming *Tess*," *Literature/Film Quarterly* 9 (1981):71–78; A. Rissik, "Laurels for the Hardy—But Less for *Tess*," *Films Illustrated* 10 (June 1981):352–55; John Simon, "Illustrated Lectures—*Tess*," *National Review* 33 (1981):501–2; and Stanley Kauffmann, "Mixed Blessings," *New Republic*, January 3 and 10, 1981, pp. 20–21.
5. Thomas Hardy, *Tess of the D'Urbervilles*, ed. Scott Elledge (New York: W. W. Norton, 1979), p. 105. All subsequent page references in the text are to this edition.
6. "Tess," *Cinéma Français*, no. 25 (1978):42.
7. See especially Dorothy Van Ghent, "On *Tess of the D'Urbervilles*," in Elledge, *Tess*, pp. 427–38; and J. Hillis Miller, *Thomas Hardy: Distance and Desire* (Cambridge, Mass.: Harvard University Press, 1970).
8. Malcolm Bradbury and James Macfarlane, "The Name and Nature of Modernism," in Malcolm Bradbury and James Macfarlane, eds., *Modernism* (London: Penguin, 1976), p 10
9. The film's conversion of theological issues into social and psychological ones was noted by Richard A. Blake: "Film Determinism," *America* 144 (n.d.):83–84.
10. See Joan Grundy, *Hardy and the Sister Arts* (New York: Barnes & Noble, 1979), for a full discussion of these allusions in the novel.
11. Donald Davidson, "The Traditional Basis of Thomas Hardy's Fiction." Reprinted in Elledge, *Tess*, p. 413.
12. Other thematic implications of Hardy's tentatively open-ended conclusion have been discussed in Alan Friedman's *The Turn of the Novel* (New York: Oxford, 1966), pp. 51–65.
13. "Tess," p. 40.
14. See especially Arnold Kettle, "Introduction to *Tess of the D'Urbervilles*" in Albert A. LaValley, ed., *Twentieth Century Views of "Tess of the D'Urbervilles"* (Englewood Cliffs, N.J.: Prentice-Hall, 1969), pp. 14–29.
15. Irving Howe, "*Tess of the D'Urbervilles:* At the Center of Hardy's Achievement," reprinted in Elledge, *Tess*, p. 454.
16. Jane Marcus has argued that Tess is more passive in the film than in the novel because her attempt to baptize her baby and her murder of Alec are not shown ("A Tess for Child-Molesters," p. 3). My own argument suggests other reasons for these omissions and emphasizes the film's attention to Tess's own sexual desires.
17. Elaine Showalter, "Victorian Women and Insanity," *Victorian Studies* 23, no. 2 (Winter 1980):173. The sexist presumptions in the book have often been noted. See Mary Ann Childers, "Thomas Hardy, The Man Who 'Liked' Women,"

Criticism 23 (Fall 1981):317–34, for a recent discussion of this issue in Hardy's novel.

18. Elizabeth Hardwick, *Seduction and Betrayal: Women and Literature* (New York: Random House, 1975), p. 185.

19. This similarity between the two men led D. H. Lawrence to conclude that Alec was more suited to Tess than Angel, because Alec experienced fewer conflicts about asserting his sexual dominance over her. See "The Male and Female Principles in *Tess of the D'Urbervilles*" in Elledge, *Tess*, pp. 406–14.

20. Carolyn Heilbrun, *Toward a Definition of Androgyny* (New York: Knopf, 1973).

21. For a discussion of this relationship see Edmund Wilson's *Axel's Castle* (New York: Charles Scribner & Sons, 1931), p. 23 et passim.

22. "*Tess*," p. 41.

Selected Bibliography

Note: all major bibliographic sources before 1979 are annotated in *Roman Polanski: A Guide to References and Resources*, listed immediately below.

1. Books

Bisplinghoff, Gretchen, and **Wexman, Virginia Wright.** *Roman Polanski: A Guide to References and Resources.* Boston: G. K. Hall, 1979, 116 pp. A predominantly bibliographic project, with brief biographical and critical sketches followed by complete credits and plot summaries of all Polanski's films through *The Tenant.* An extensive annotated bibliography of writing about the director includes foreign language sources.

Kiernan, Thomas. *The Roman Polanski Story.* New York: Grove Press, 1980, 262 pp. A sensationalized biography that focuses on Polanski's trial for unlawful sexual relations with a minor.

Leaming, Barbara. *Polanski: The Filmmaker as Voyeur.* New York: Simon & Schuster, 1982, 220 pp. A thoroughly researched critical biography that both gains and loses from the fact that the subject has not cooperated with the author. The films are discussed as expressions of Polanski's exhibitionistic personality.

Polanski, Roman. *Roman.* New York: William Morrow, 1984, 461 pp. Most useful for its lengthy discussion of the author's early years.

2. Parts of books

Cawelti, John G. *"Chinatown* and Generic Transformation in Recent American Films."* In *Film Theory and Criticism,* 2d ed. Edited by Gerald Mast and Marshall Cohen. New York: Oxford, 1979, pp. 559–79. A scholar of popular culture analyzes *Chinatown* as part of a growing trend in Hollywood filmmaking that self-consciously treats the nature of the generic experience.

Manvell, Roger. *Theater and Film.* Cranbury, N.J.: A. S. Barnes, 1979, pp. 151–64. An analysis of Polanski's Shakespeare adaptation that stresses the romantic attachment between the Macbeths.

Murphy, Michael. *The Celluloid Vampires.* Ann Arbor: Pierian Press, 1979, pp. 114, 116–18, 225. *Dance of the Vampires* is briefly discussed in relation to other vampire films. Its unusual ending, in which evil triumphs over good, is stressed.

Tuska, Jon. *The Detective in Hollywood.* Garden City, N.Y.: Doubleday, 1978, pp. 401–10. An anecdotal discussion of *Chinatown* in relation to earlier detec-

tive films. Contains quotations from the director on the changes he made in
the original ending.

3. Articles

Costanzo, William V. "Polanski in Essex Filming *Tess of the D'Urbervilles*." *Literature/Film Quarterly* 9 (1981):71–78. Review finds Polanski's adaptation too lethargic as a result of its "realistic" presentation of romantic sentiments.

Glazer, Mitchell. "On the Lam with Roman Polanski." *Rolling Stone*, April 20, 1981. An impressionistic portrait of Polanski's life-style in Paris, during which the director comments about politics, his past, and *Tess*.

Harmetz, Aljean. "An Interview with Roman Polanski." *New York Times*, December 11, 1980, p. 69. Polanski discusses his newest film as an expression of his newly softened sensibility.

Lawton, Anna. "The Double: A Doestoevskian Theme in Polanski." *Literature/Film Quarterly* 9 (1981):121–29. The doppelgänger motif in *Knife in the Water* and *Dance of the Vampires* is analyzed in terms of how it reveals the "moral laxity" of the protagonists.

Linderman, Deborah. "Oedipus in Chinatown." *Enclitic* 5 (Fall 1981):190–203. The film's references to the myth of Oedipus are related to the oedipal nature of its own narrative, when considered from a Freudian perspective.

Marcus, Jane. "A *Tess* for Child Molesters." *Jump/Cut*, no. 26 (1981):3. Polanski's sexist attitudes are seen as reflected in the passivity and victimization of his heroine.

Middleton, David. "The Self-Reflexive Nature of Polanski's *Macbeth*." *University of Dayton Review* 14, no. 1 (Winter 1979–80):89–94. A discussion of the self-conscious devices in the film combined with an interview with the director.

Wexman, Virginia Wright. "*Macbeth* and Polanski's Theme of Regression." *University of Dayton Review* 14, no. 1 (Winter 1979–80):85–88. The film is considered as an expression of the psychological state of its hero.

Williams, Linda. "Polanski's *The Tenant* and Films about Madness." *Cinema Journal* 20, no. 2 (Spring 1981):63–73. The film is considered in relation to surrealistic techniques of depicting insanity.

Filmography

TWO MEN AND A WARDROBE [*Dwaj Ludzie Z Szasa*] (Polish Film Academy, Lodz, 1958)
Screenplay: Roman Polanski
Cinematographer: Maciej Kijowski
Music: Krzysztof Komeda-Trzcinski
Cast: Henryk Kluba, Jakub Goldberg, Roman Polanski
Running time: 15 minutes
16mm rental: Contemporary

WHEN ANGELS FALL [*Gdy Spadaja Anioly*] (1959)
Screenplay: Roman Polanski
Cinematographer: Henryk Kucharski
Music: Krzysztof Komeda-Trzcinski
Cast: Barbara Kwiatkowska, Jakub Goldberg, Roman Polanski, Henryk Kluba
Running time: 22 minutes

THE FAT AND THE LEAN [*Le Gros et Le Maigre*] (Claude Joudioux/A.P.E.C. [Paris], 1961)
Producer: Claude Joudioux
Screenplay: Roman Polanski, Jean-Pierre Rousseau
Cinematographer: Jean-Michel Trzcinski
Music: Krzysztof Komeda-Trzcinski
Cast: Roman Polanski, Andre Katelbach
Running time: 16 minutes

KNIFE IN THE WATER [*Noz W Wodzie*] (Kamera film Unit for film Polski, 1962)
Producer: Stanislaw Zylewicz
Screenplay: Jerzy Skolimowski, Jakub Goldberg, Roman Polanski
Cinematographer: Jerzy Lipman
Music: Krzysztof Komeda-Trzcinski
Sound: Halina Paszkowska
Editor: Halina Prugar
Cast: Neon Niemczyk (Andrzej), Jolanta Umecka (Krystyna), Zygmunt Malanawicz (Youth)

Running time: 94 minutes
Premier: October 28, 1963, New York City
16mm rental: Kanawha Films

MAMMALS [*Ssaki*] (Studio Se-Ma-For, Lodz, 1962)
Screenplay: A Kondraciuk, Roman Polanski
Cinematographer: Andrzej Kostenko
Music: Krzysztof Komeda-Trzcinski
Editors: Halina Prugar, J. Niedzwiedzka
Cast: Henryk Kluba, Michal Zolnierkiewcz
Running time: 11 minutes
16mm rental: Connoisseur

REPULSION (Compton/Tekli Film Productions, 1965)
Producer: Gene Gutowski
Screenplay: Roman Polanski, Gerard Brach
Cinematography: Gilbert Taylor
Art Director: Seamus Flannery
Music: Chico Hamilton
Sound Editor: Tom Priestly
Editor: Alastair McIntyre
Cast: Catherine Deneuve (Carol), Ian Hendry (Michael), John Fraser (Colin),
Yvonne Furneaux (Helen), Patrick Wymark (Landlord), Renee Houston (Miss
Balch)
Running time: 104 minutes
Premier: October 3, 1965
16mm rental: Royal Films International

CUL-DE-SAC (Compton/Tekli Film Productions, 1966)
Producer: Gene Gutowski
Screenplay: Roman Polanski, Gerard Brach
Cinematographer: Gilbert Taylor, B.S.C.
Art Director: George Lack
Production Designer: Voytek
Costumes: Bridget Sellers
Music: Krzysztof Komeda-Trzcinski
Sound: David Campling
Editor: Alastair McIntyre
Cast: Donald Pleasance (George), Françoise Dorleac (Teresa), Lionel Stander
(Richard), Jack MacGowran (Albert)
Running time: 107 minutes
Premier: November 7, 1966
16mm rental: Sigma III Corporation

DANCE OF THE VAMPIRES [also: *The Fearless Vampire Killers or Pardon
Me, But Your Teeth Are in My Neck*] (Cadre Films-Filmways, Incorporated,
1967)
Producer: Gene Gutowski
Assistant Director: Roy Stevens

Screenplay: Gerard Brach, Roman Polanski
Cinematographer: Douglas Slocombe
Art Director: Fred Carter
Production Designer: Wilfred Shingleton
Costumes: Sophie Devine
Music: Krzysztof Komeda-Trzcinski
Sound: Lionel Selwyn
Editor: Alastair McIntyre
Cast: Jack MacGowran (Professor Abronsious), Roman Polanski (Alfred), Alfie
Bass (Shagal), Jessie Robins (Rebecca), Sharon Tate (Sarah), Ferdy Mayne (Count
Von Krolock)
Running time: 91 minutes (first version, 107 minutes)
Premier: November 13, 1967
16mm rental: Metro-Goldwyn-Mayer

ROSEMARY'S BABY (Paramount Pictures, 1968)
Producer: William Castle
Assistant Director: Daniel J. McCauley
Screenplay: Roman Polanski, from Ira Levin's novel *Rosemary's Baby*
Cinematographer: William Fraker
Art Director: Joel Schiller
Production Designer: Richard Sylbert
Set Decoration: Robert Nelson
Costumes: Anthea Sylbert
Music: Krzysztof Komeda-Trzcinski
Sound: Harold Lewis, John Wilkinson
Special Effects: Farciot Edouart
Editors: Sam O'Steen, Robert Wyman
Cast: Mia Farrow (Rosemary Woodhouse), John Cassavetes (Guy Woodhouse),
Ruth Gordon (Minnie Castevet), Sidney Blackmer (Roman Castevet), Maurice
Evans (Hutch), Ralph Bellamy (Dr. Sapirstein)
Running time: 137 minutes
Premier: June 12, 1968
16mm rental: Films Inc.

MACBETH (Playboy Productions/Caliban Films, 1971)
Producer: Andrew Braunsberg
Assistant Director: Simon Relph
Screenplay: Roman Polanski, Kenneth Tynan, from William Shakespeare's
Macbeth
Cinematographer: Gil Taylor
Art Director: Fred Carter
Production Designer: Wilfrid Shingleton
Set Decorator: Bryan Braves
Costumes: Anthony Mendleson
Music: Third Ear Band
Sound: Simon Kaye
Special Effects: Ted Samuels
Editor: Alastair McIntyre

Cast: John Finch (Macbeth), Francesca Annis (Lady Macbeth), Martin Shaw (Banquo), Nicholas Selby (Duncan), John Stride (Ross), Stephan Chase (Malcolm), Paul Shelley (Donalbain), Terence Bayer (Macduff), Diane Fletcher (Lady Macduff)
Running time: 140 minutes
Premier: December 8, 1971
16mm rental: Swank

WHAT? [*Che?*] (C. C. Champion [Rome]/Les Films Concordia [Paris]/Dieter Geissler Produktion [Munich], 1973)
Producer: Carlo Ponti
Assistant Director: Antonio Brandt
Screenplay: Gerard Brach, Roman Polanski
Cinematographers: Marcello Gatti, Giuseppe Ruzzolini
Art Director: Franco Fumagalli
Production Designer: Aurelio Crugnola
Costumes: Adriana Berselli
Music: Claudio Gizzi
Sound: Piero Fondi
Editor: Alastair McIntyre
Cast: Sydne Rome (Nancy), Marcello Mastroianni (Alex), Hugh Griffith (Joseph Noblart), Romolo Valli (Giovanni), Guido Alberti (Priest), Gianfranco Piacentini (Tony), Roger Middleton (Jimmy), Roman Polanski (Mosquito)
Running time: 112 minutes
Premier: October 3, 1973
16mm rental: Avco Embassy Pictures

CHINATOWN (Long Road Productions; Paramount-Penthouse Presentation, 1974)
Producer: Robert Evans
Assistant Directors: Howard W. Koch, Jr., Michele Ader
Screenplay: Robert Towne
Cinematographer: John A. Alonzo
Art Director: W. Stewart Campbell
Set Designers: Gabe Resh, Robert Resh
Production Designer: Richard Sylbert
Costumes: Anthea Sylbert
Music: Jerry Goldsmith
Sound Editor: Robert Cornett
Editor: Sam O'Steen
Cast: Jack Nicholson (J. J. Gittes), Faye Dunaway (Evelyn Mulwray), John Huston (Noah Cross), Perry Lopez (Escobar), John Hillerman (Yelburton), Darrell Zwerling (Hollis Mulwray), Diane Ladd (Ida Sessions), Roy Jenson (Mulvihill), Roman Polanski (Man with knife)
Running time: 130 minutes
Premier: June 17, 1974
16mm rental: Paramount Pictures

THE TENANT [*Le Locataire*] (1976)
Producer: Andrew Braunsberg
Assistant Director: Marc Greenbaum
Screenplay: Gerard Brach, Roman Polanski
Cinematographer: Sven Nykvist, A.S.C.
Art Directors: Claude Moesching, Albert Rajau
Production Designer: Pierre Guffroy
Costumes: Mimi Gayo
Music: Phillippe Sarde
Sound Editor: Michele Boehm
Editor: Francoise Bonnot
Cast: Roman Polanski (Trelkovsky), Isabelle Adjani (Stella), Shelley Winters (The Concierge), Melvyn Douglas (M. Zy), Jo Van Fleet (Mme. Dioz), Bernard Fresson (Scope), Lila Kedrova (Mme. Gaderian)
Running time: 126 minutes
16mm rental: ClC

TESS (Renn Productions [France] and Burrill Productions [England], 1980)
Producer: Claude Berri
Screenplay: Gerard Brach, Roman Polanski, and John Brownjohn, based on the novel by Thomas Hardy
Cinematographers: Geoffrey Unsworth, B.S.C., Ghislain Cloquet, A.S.C.
Art Director: Jack Stephens
Production Designer: Pierre Guffroy
Costumes: Anthony Powell
Music: Philippe Sarde
Sound Editor: Jean-Pierre Ruh
Editors: Alastair McIntyre, Tom Priestley
Cast: Nastassia Kinski (Tess), Peter Firth (Angel Clare), Leigh Lawson (Alex d'Urberville), John Collin (John Durbeyfield), Arielle Dombasle (Mercy Chant)
Running time: 190 minutes
Premier: December 12, 1980
16mm rental: Columbia Pictures

Index